G000109502

PREPARING
FOR YOUR
MOVE ABROAD

PREPARING FOR YOUR MOVE ABROAD

Relocating, Settling In, and Managing Culture Shock

Rona Hart, Ph.D.

·K·U·P·E·R·A·R·D·

ISBN 978 1 85733 644 3
Also available as an e-book: eISBN 978 1 85733 650 4

British Library Cataloguing in Publication Data
A CIP catalogue entry for this book is available from the
British Library

First published in Great Britain 2012
by Kuperard, an imprint of Bravo Ltd
59 Hutton Grove, London N12 8DS
Tel: +44 (0) 20 8446 2440   Fax: +44 (0) 20 8446 2441
www.culturesmart.co.uk
Inquiries: sales@kuperard.co.uk

Distributed in the United States and Canada
by Random House Distribution Services
1745 Broadway, New York, NY 10019
Tel: +1 (212) 572-2844   Fax: +1 (212) 572-4961
Inquiries: csorders@randomhouse.com

Editor Geoffrey Chesler
Design Bobby Birchall

Printed in Singapore

Cover images and illustration on page 84 © iStockphoto

ABOUT THE AUTHOR

RONA HART is an academic researcher, trainer, and counselor. She has a doctorate from King's College London in Education (Social Psychology) and a Post-Graduate Diploma in Group Facilitation and Counseling (TELEM).

After completing her Ph.D. on immigration, relocation, and cross-cultural experience, she developed a series of techniques and interventions, based on the principles of Positive Psychology, that are designed to facilitate major life transitions and desired transformations. Later she established a successful company offering relocation training and counseling services.

Dr. Hart is an expert in the psychology of change. She has devoted her career to empowering people, helping them to shift unproductive thoughts and behaviors into successful patterns that allow them to generate positive outcomes and transform their lives.

CONTENTS

PART 2: CROSSING CULTURES EFFECTIVELY

PART 3: ON THE MOVE

PART 4: THE UPS AND DOWNS OF ADJUSTMENT

PART 5: UNDER THE SPOTLIGHT: THE CULTURE-SHOCK EXPERIENCE

INTRODUCTION

Welcome to *Preparing For Your Move Abroad*—your personal relocation training program!

International relocation is, unquestionably, one of the most exciting and rewarding ventures you will ever embark upon. It is also one of the most challenging, and, indeed, life-changing experiences. Every aspect of your life will be affected by this move.

The sunny side of relocation is well known. For some, it may well be a path to survival. For many, it is a quest for progress: better jobs or educational opportunities, an improved lifestyle, new relationships, and new dreams and goals to accomplish.

The cloudy side of relocation has also been acknowledged. No matter how successful the move turns out to be, most people who relocate experience pressures and challenges that tax them, both physically and emotionally.

This book is a complete relocation guide that brings the practical details of the relocation journey together with the cultural and psychological aspects. It provides you with more than knowledge: it provides a success plan—a series of easy to follow, step-by-step guides that will help you to prepare for and manage the tasks and challenges involved in your move abroad effectively.

My goal in writing this book is to turn challenges into opportunities for growth. I believe the more knowledge you have, and the more prepared and better equipped you are to address the challenges of your relocation, the more effective and successful you will be in confronting and responding to these challenges. The book provides a tried and tested set of tools that will enable you to go through your journey with clarity, confidence, and peace of mind, and make your transition fruitful, efficient, and rewarding.

Learning to manage change will make you a better qualified professional, equipped with a cross-cultural mindset that will enable you to understand and manage difference anywhere in the world. This book shows you how.

Preparing For Your Move Abroad is organized along a typical relocation timeline. It takes you from the very first stage of your relocation—the decision to move—to your integration into the host society, and through each and every stage in between.

The first part of the book is about preparation. It lays down a strategy for efficient and timely decision making, planning, and preparation, that is practical and easy to follow.

The second part concentrates on the cultural aspect of your move. It discusses what culture is, explains the cross-cultural adaptation process and why crossing cultures provokes culture shock, and offers you a framework for cross-cultural learning.

The third part concentrates on the transition period of your relocation journey, from the shipment of your belongings to the relocation day.

The fourth part looks into the settling-in and adjustment period, and takes you, step by step, through the process of reorganizing your life.

The fifth part provides you with essential knowledge about culture shock: what is it, why it occurs, what triggers it, and its phases and symptoms.

Finally, the sixth part reviews the adaptation to integration phases, and offers a knowledge base and powerful strategies for bridging the cultural divide.

In short, *Preparing For Your Move Abroad* offers:
+ A strong knowledge base on each and every phase of the relocation journey.
+ A strategy to manage the issues at hand.
+ Psychological preparation.
+ An action plan, presented through exercises, action steps, check lists, and many easy-to-use tools.

Follow these signposts to help you navigate your way through the book:
+ Essential knowledge and useful tips
✍ Exercises
❑ Action steps (presented as check lists)

The book is intended for three groups of people:
+ Settlers: those of you who are relocating with the intention of settling permanently in your destination country.
+ Sojourners: those who are relocating abroad for a period of a year or more with the intention of returning to your homelands in due course (such as expatriates, academics on sabbatical, overseas students, volunteers, and others).
+ Relocation professionals: if you are a relocation agent, a counselor, a trainer, a psychologist, or a social worker, working with people who have relocated or who are planning to relocate, you can use this guide as a source of ideas to work with individuals or groups.

Before we go ahead, you may want to know something about me. I am a researcher and a relocation trainer working with bright, successful professional people—mainly expatriates and immigrants—to prepare them and their families for their move abroad.

My personal relocation experience is rather unusual. I have moved homes twenty-four times, and have experienced, both as a teen and as an adult, six international moves and four re-entries. Importantly, I went, together with my husband and two children, through all the ups and downs of the immigration and naturalization experience, as we finally decided to make Britain our permanent home.

With this experience, it is probably no coincidence that I chose to devote nearly a decade of my life to conducting several studies (including my Ph.D.) on the relocation experience, exploring its social and psychological aspects.

After completing my Ph.D., I searched for ways to make my knowledge useful to others, and to help facilitate and alleviate the challenges of relocation. I went on to establish a company that offers relocation training and counseling services.

I am delighted to be able to share with you the best methods and tools that I have developed, tested, and perfected over the years, through my research, training, and counseling programs.

I have written this book after having myself experienced a "crash landing" followed by severe culture shock, which cost me and my family dearly in terms of time, money, missed opportunities, bitter moods, and severed relationships. This was when we moved to the UK. Despite my previous relocation experience, it took me nearly three years to recover. Indeed, as I have learned—the hard way—having the experience of moving and living abroad does not necessarily mean understanding it or learning from it. I wish I had known then what I know and teach today, and I sincerely hope that I can save you the agony and the losses that I have experienced and incurred.

I see this book as a training program, and I have set it up like a seminar or a session, just as if you came to me as a private client, or participated in one of my training programs.

The knowledge and guidance provided here are drawn mainly from my training programs, from current research into the relocation experience, and into the psychology of change, as well as from my own experiences and the learning that I have gained from them.

In addition, the book contains stories quoted from people who have been through this journey. Some were my clients; others participated in my research. Their accounts present both the excitement and the satisfaction they experienced, along with the confusion and frustration that are all part of this journey.

This is not necessarily a book to be read from cover to cover. It is a reference and a source book that you can dip into. You can look for the phase or problem that you are currently going through, complete the exercises, acquire the relevant knowledge, apply the strategies, and move on. Use the pages to write on, and feel free to use the book as a notebook.

A word of caution is due here before we dive in. It may be tempting to think there is some magic pill that can remove all the challenges and hurdles involved in relocation: the "right" way to do this; a simple list of dos and don'ts. But experience has taught me that relocation is a very personal process, in which context rules, and yet, our perspective, mindset, and, indeed, our psychology, matter more than anything else. A list of "to dos" and a detailed description of the host country and culture can only take us so far. This book offers guidance and detailed "to dos," but it is mainly designed to help you develop the mindset and the skills that will enable you to function "outside the script."

I hope that this book will motivate and inspire you through your intercultural journey, and make you question and challenge your own thinking about yourself and others as you settle in and move more deeply into the host culture around you.

My personal goal as your trainer is to empower you, so that you will be able to go on your relocation journey with energy and drive, a positive outlook, passion, and joy, knowing exactly what lies ahead and having the tools and strategies to address whatever shows up, effectively, calmly, and with confidence. My promise to you is that you will find here both the knowledge and the means to make your relocation a huge success.

I hope you are ready for an inspiring journey. Fasten your seat belts—here we go!

Chapter 1

DECISIONS, DECISIONS

> The decision-making phase is the most crucial stage
> of your move, which determines the quality of
> your entire relocation journey.
> This is because it shapes your mindset, and
> therefore your capacity to handle the challenges involved.

The decision to relocate often takes place six months to a year prior to the move. However, the deliberation phase leading to the decision can vary significantly. I have met people who discussed and mulled over their decision for years, and others who spent just a few hours or days thinking about it.

If you have made a hasty decision, are unsure about your relocation, are unwillingly trailing behind an enthusiastic spouse or colleague, or pulling along an unhappy teenager, this will undoubtedly influence your attitude, resilience, and capacity to deal with the challenges you may meet. It will also affect your ability to bear the emotional strains of the culture-shock phase.

It is extremely important, then, that you and everyone around you make an informed decision regarding your move, and a committed one, that will carry you through the more taxing times of your journey.

In my line of work, I have met many people who relocated abroad having based their decision on vague dreams and unrealistic expectations. I have also met people who moved abroad without ever making a resolute decision about their move or what they wanted to gain from their time abroad. The outcomes of such attitudes can be unpleasant, and even disastrous.

> Moving abroad without making an informed and committed decision, with vague goals, no goals, or unrealistic expectations, is one of the main causes of culture shock and relocation failure.

The story below demonstrates the possible costs of uncommitted decisions.

Where Are Your Mental Suitcases?
Renni's Story

When we moved to London, I was the typical "trailing spouse." Actually, perhaps I was not so typical, because I really didn't want to come. I was reluctantly, and even resentfully, dragged behind my husband on his first expatriate mission. He was so proud and happy to get this position that I just couldn't tell him how I felt, and I definitely didn't want to spoil it for him.

My life in Israel was good. I had a senior job, which I loved, in a government department, and was expecting to become head of the department that year. We had a lovely home, a lovely family life, and the children were happy. I had no reason to leave.

So I came to London not only unprepared for this experience, but also unwilling to put in any real effort to make it work. For the next two years I lived here "on hold," as if I had taken a break from life—I was physically here, but my heart was back home. Everything I did in London was "temporary," and I was simply waiting to go back, three years down the line.

I hated everything about life in London, and was constantly moaning about the weather, the house, the schools, the cost of things, the TV, the food, the English people. You name it—I found something wrong with it.

Then I met Rona, and went to her Culture-Shock workshop in an attempt to understand what was happening to me. In the course of the workshop, she asked:

"Have you made a committed decision about your relocation?"

"What attitude have you brought with you?"

"Are these attitudes supporting or hindering your decision?"

Then it hit me! I realized that as a result of my lack of commitment, I had adopted an attitude to our life here that not only weighed us down but really soured our entire stay here, and our relationship too.

"Where are your mental suitcases?" she continued. "Have you unpacked them?"

I realized that my mental suitcases had been sitting by the door for the last two years! I had never really unpacked them. I had not opened up to what living in London had to offer us, and I had made no effort to make our life here work.

As a result of my lack of decision and negative attitude, I had no resilience. When difficulties and hurdles appeared—and they did—I simply could not handle them. The smallest problem would make me cry: "This is just too hard. I'm going back home on the first flight!"

Finally—two years after my relocation—I was ready to make the decision, and play to the full!

Decisions and attitudes matter! I therefore urge you to make an informed and committed decision regarding your relocation, which will carry you through the more challenging times, and enable you to settle in psychologically.

There are many reasons for wanting to relocate abroad. Your own motives may have to do with career aspirations, finances, education, environment, lifestyle preferences, health, relationships, family matters, or simply your own or your family's general well-being.

Relocating abroad can certainly lead to positive life changes, and yet your relocation may not instantly bring those desired changes. It is therefore essential to examine your motives and clarify your goals, and then consider carefully whether these goals are attainable in your desired destination and in your given time frame.

There are four main steps in the decision-making process:
+ Setting your relocation goals.
+ Researching your destination country, and seeking information that will enable you to assess whether your goals are realistic and attainable there.
+ Weighing up the rewards of your relocation against the short- and long-term costs of your move.
+ Making a committed decision based on your findings.

The following exercises will help you to make an educated and resolute decision.

✍ RELOCATION GOAL-SETTING EXERCISE

The momentum of our daily lives rarely allows us to take the time we need to think about our dreams and goals. The prospect of relocating gives us an opportunity to take a fresh look at life, and to set ourselves some goals!

Goal-setting is an extremely powerful tool for decision-making. Not only does it enable you to understand the things that are most important to you, and exactly what you want to achieve by relocating, but it also gives you a clearer view about how you can achieve your ambitions.

Clarifying why you wish to relocate and writing down your relocation goals is an important starting point. This exercise is designed to help you formulate and articulate those goals and to examine why you wish to relocate.

1. What are your relocation goals? What do you want to achieve by relocating to your chosen destination? Consider the following areas of your life: career, education, lifestyle, finances, family life, relationships with significant others, health, hobbies and leisure activities, social life, community, spirituality, self-development, and your psychological state.
(i) List your relocation goals in the table below.
(ii) When do you want to achieve your goal? Write a future date next to each goal.

Relocation Goals	Date

decisions, decisions

2. Why do you want to achieve these goals? Why are they important to you? What will the benefits of achieving them be to you?

3. How will you know you have succeeded in achieving your goals? What event or moment will mark the achievement of your goals?

4. How would you feel if you achieved these goals?

5. How would you feel if you did not achieve these goals?

6. Now consider this question carefully. Can you achieve these goals without relocating?

✍️ REALITY CHECK EXERCISE

Now that you have clarified your relocation goals, it is crucial to conduct a reality check.

This exercise is designed to help you research and assess whether your relocation goals are achievable at your chosen destination, within your time frame.

Once you have ensured that you can achieve the goals that you have set for your relocation, you can make a more informed and committed decision.

Fill out the following template for each of your goals.

1. Write your relocation goal below.

----

2. Now consider: is this goal attainable in your chosen destination?

----

3. Is this goal achievable within your set timeframe?

----

4. If you are not clear whether you can achieve this goal in your destination country, or within your timeframe, consider what information you require in order to gain more clarity. To help you conduct your search for information more effectively, refer to Chapter 3.

Note down the type of information you require, and where you can find it.

Information Required	Source of information

Take the time to find the information you require, study it, and carefully evaluate your goals and expectations. Are they realistic?

ASSESSING THE REWARDS OF YOUR RELOCATION AGAINST THE COSTS

This exercise is designed to help you examine the likely benefits and costs of your relocation, both to you and to others around you.

1. What would be the rewards of successful relocation to you and to those around you?

2. Relocation requires investment of time, money, effort, and other resources. What would you need to invest or learn in order to achieve your relocation goals?

_____

_____

_____

_____

_____

_____

_____

_____

_____

3. What would be the cost, to you and others, of relocating and achieving these goals? Consider all the costs, in terms of finance, time, effort, relationships, and emotion. Examine short-term costs connected with the move itself, and long-term costs.

Short-term costs:

_____

_____

_____

_____

_____

_____

Long-term costs:

_____

_____

_____

_____

_____

4. Do the rewards outweigh the costs?

5. What would be the cost of not relocating? What would be the cost of not achieving these goals?

6. Are your relocation goals ethical and fair for those around you?

7. Are these goals in accord with your other life goals?

preparing for your move abroad

 IT'S DECISION TIME!

To help you analyze your own motivations and considerations for relocation, we will be looking at four factors:

Pull factors:
What is pulling you toward your destination country? What would be the benefits of this move?

Push factors:
What makes you want to leave your current way of life and place of residence?

Stay factors:
What are the things that make you want to stay in your current place of residence?

Deterring factors:
What would be the costs and risks involved in moving to and living in your destination country?

   Now analyze your motivations to relocate. First, look at your Pull factors, and list them in the following table. Then list your Push factors, your Stay factors, and your Deterring factors.

   When the lists are complete, grade the factors in each column by their importance from 1 (not important) to 10 (very important). Add up your scores and find the total for each column.

Pull factors	Score	Push factors	Score
Total		**Total**	

Stay factors	Score	Deterring factors	Score
Total		**Total**	

The last step is to add the following scores:

Pull + Push factors   =   _____

Stay + Deterring factors   =   _____

If your Push + Pull factor score is higher than your
Stay + Deterring factor score, this means that you have
stronger reasons to relocate than to stay.

What have you learned from these exercises?

_____

_____

_____

_____

_____

Now it's time to make that decision! Are you committed to relocating and achieving your goals? Yes / No

How committed are you to achieving your relocation goals, on a scale of 1 (not committed) to 10 (very committed)?

_____

Moving doesn't start with packing boxes. It begins here, when the idea comes into your head, when you deliberate on it, and when you make that all-important decision. It is vitally important to ensure you have explored the full range of your reasons to relocate. Question whether moving will really enable you to fulfill your desired goals, or to solve the problem you may be facing, and carefully consider other options. Take time to research, gather information, and consider the benefits and rewards of your move, as well as the costs of your relocation to yourself and others. Then you are in a position to make a realistic, well-informed, win-win decision.

After reading this chapter and doing the exercises you may decide that moving is unwise at this point in time. That's fine. Even if you decide against a geographical move, you will have made a positive psychological move, simply by arriving at a decision and knowing it is the right one.

If you are now certain that you are going to relocate, make sure that those who may be accompanying you—your spouse, children, or others—are willing to move, and help them to formulate their own relocation goals. These may be entirely different from yours.

Chapter 2

RELOCATION PLANNING MADE SIMPLE

Once you have made the decision to relocate abroad, your overseas adventure is about to begin! Get ready for excitement, travel, and adventure, as well as all the work of preparing, moving, settling in, learning, and adapting.

> Never underestimate the importance of planning and preparation. Even if you are an experienced traveler, with several international moves under your belt, thorough planning and preparation are a must.

Often what determines the difference between success and failure when it comes to relocation is the amount of chaos and resulting stress that people experience as they go through the successive phases of their relocation journey. And, not surprisingly, planning can make a huge difference in alleviating stress and minimizing disorder.

THE BENEFITS OF PLANNING

✦ Planning enables you to manage the big tasks involved in your relocation without the stress.

✦ It helps you to create a focus and a sense of direction at a time when there is some turbulence and uncertainty in your life.

✦ It enables you to maintain confidence, energy, and a positive attitude at a time when your life skills and knowledge are being challenged.

✦ A good plan encourages you to act at times when you find it difficult to do so.

✦ It brings order, structure, and comfort into your life at a time when your routines are interrupted and changing and you may feel out of tune.

✦ One of the major causes of culture shock is unrealistic expectations. Thorough planning helps you to develop more realistic expectations of your life in the new place, thereby preventing and moderating the culture-shock experience.

✦ Planning ahead helps you to avoid costly mistakes and minimize unpleasant surprises and last-minute scrambles, thereby reducing stress and panic.

✦ A well-planned move can ease the psychological strains involved in your relocation, while a poorly planned move can add to your stress just when you need it least.

One of the main differences between people who have turned their relocation dream into reality and those who continue to talk and dream about it is in the planning. Why? Simply because planning makes it all possible, it makes it real, and, more importantly, it relieves the fear and the doubts.

THE RELOCATION JOURNEY TYPICALLY CONSISTS OF THE FOLLOWING PHASES

✦ The pre-relocation period:
  • Deliberation and decision
  • Preparation and planning
  • Farewell
  • The transition
  • The relocation day
✦ The post-relocation period, which also marks the beginning of the cross-cultural adaptation process, typically includes:
  • The honeymoon phase
  • The culture-shock period
  • Recovery, adaptation, and growth
  • Integration

As soon as you set your date for relocation, draw up a relocation plan. The main goal of your plan is to manage the logistics of your move in an orderly and timely way, as well as to support your adjustment to your new environment and help you to set up your new life routines quickly.

The first step is to create a map—an outline for your entire relocation journey. The next step is to break down each phase and plan it in detail.

✍ DRAWING A MAP OF YOUR JOURNEY

Before you go into any detailed planning, it is essential to sketch a general outline of your entire journey. The purpose of this exercise is to help you formulate a mental picture, or an overview, of the journey, along its timeline.

Your map will show you the way from the beginning to a chosen point in your journey—preferably several months after the settling-in period—and will highlight the main junctions you will need to cross.

You will require a planner, or diary, for this exercise, or you can use a computer or phone planner.

1. Identify the main events of your relocation journey, from today to a year after your move, or later if necessary. Write them in the following table, with their dates.

The events might include: moving out of your home, pre-relocation training sessions, the shipping day, farewell parties, the relocation day, the move into permanent accommodation, the first day of work, the arrival of the shipment.

Events	Date

2. Schedule all these dates in your planner or diary. If you don't yet have dates for some of the events, try to estimate when, roughly, they are likely to take place.

3. List in the table below any events over which you have no control, and which are likely to affect your relocation timetable. Consider events such as public holidays (in both countries), work or project schedules, family events, exam days, end of school, first day of school.

Events	Date

4. Now schedule these dates in your planner.

Your journey map is beginning to come together now. All that is left is to schedule the preparation activities that precede each of the main relocation events.

5. In the following table, identify the events that require preparation and action. Write their dates next to them. Assess how long it should take you to complete the preparation for each event, and note this in the third column. Then mark in the fourth column the start date for your preparation.

Events	Date	Preparation time required	Start to prepare on

6. Schedule the preparation period for each event in your planner.

Your journey map is now complete!

EASY PLANNING IN SEVEN STEPS
Planning your relocation is fairly similar to planning other large projects in business or life. Here are some simple steps and tips you can follow to plan your relocation process:

+ Define the areas that require planning.
+ Identify the main tasks in each area.
+ Highlight the decisions to be made—and make these decisions!
+ Identify the information that is required.
+ Plan each task: break it into small action steps.
+ Schedule the action steps in your planner.
+ Act on your plan!

The next exercise offers a simple yet systematic way to plan each and every aspect and stage of your move.

relocation planning made simple

EASY PLANNING EXERCISE

1. Look at the list below, and identify the aspects of life in your homeland for which you need to plan or make adjustments before your departure. Use the following list as a guideline, and add to it or delete from it items as appropriate:

- Housing

- Work

- Finances / banking

- Education

- Health

- Transportation

- Communication

- The move (paperwork, flights, farewell parties, temporary accommodation, shipment, etc.)

- Social / relationships

- Recreation

-

-

-

-

Now do the same for your destination country. Look at the list below and identify the aspects that you need to plan for in relation to your life in your new country. Use the list as a guideline, and add to it or delete from it items as appropriate:

- Legal (passports, visas, etc.)

- Housing

- Work

- Finances / banking

- Education / language learning

- Health

- Communication

- Transportation

- Social / relationships

- Recreation

- Vacations / home visits

- The move

-

-

-

2. Now look at both lists and identify the main tasks that you need to address in each area. You can use the following tables to define these tasks.

Homeland tasks	Main tasks
Housing	
Work	
Finances / banking	
Education	
Health	
Communication	
Transportation	
The move	
Social / relationships	
Recreation	

Destination country tasks	Main tasks
Legal	
Housing	
Work	
Finances / banking	
Education / language	
Health	
Communication	
Transportation	
Social / relationships	
Recreation	
Vacations /home visits	
The move	

preparing for your move abroad

Below is an example of this table as it was used by a couple who recently relocated from the UK to Spain with their two young children.

Homeland tasks	Main tasks
Housing	Complete redecoration of children's room and roof.
	Sell / rent out house.
	Notify all service providers.
Work	Complete projects x, y, z.
	Update projects folder.
	Clear office / computer.
Finances / banking	Cancel standing orders / direct debits (apart from credit cards).
Education	Notify schools.
	Collect paperwork from schools.
Health	Extend private insurance to cover first weeks abroad.
Transportation	Sell both cars.
Communication	Close house phone account.
	Keep cell phone account.
Recreation	Cancel gym and football club memberships.
Social / relationships	Notify friends and acquaintances.
	Arrange for parents to come with us for first two weeks.
The move	Arrange shipment.
	Prepare for shipment.
	Buy x, y, z.
	Arrange farewell party.
	Arrange children's parties at school.
	Purchase flight tickets.

As you can see, when the couple wrote up their plan they were unsure whether they would be selling or renting out their property. If you find yourself in a similar situation, with areas in which you have not yet decided what to do, go to Step 3. If all your relocation decisions have been made, you can skip this step and go straight to Step 4.

> **3. Using the task lists that you have created, highlight areas where there are still decisions to be made. It is important to identify these as early as possible, in order to ensure that you have enough time to make informed decisions. The purpose of this step is therefore to make you aware of these decisions, and allow you to consider all aspects of the situation before you leap into action.**
>
> Use the table below as a template when considering the decisions relating to your homeland.
>
> | Homeland tasks | Decisions |
> |---|---|
> | Housing | |
> | Work | |
> | Finances / banking | |
> | Education | |
> | Health | |
> | Communication | |
> | Transportation | |
> | Recreation | |
> | Social / relationships | |
> | The move | |

Use the table below as a template when considering the decisions relating to your destination country:

Destination country tasks	Decisions
Legal	
Housing	
Work	
Finances / banking	
Education	
Health	
Communication	
Transportation	
Social / relationships	
Recreation	
Vacations / home visits	
The move	

Here is an example:

Homeland tasks	Decisions
Housing	Sell or rent out our property?
Work	Leave my job now, or commute until I find a job in the destination country?
Finances / banking	Close bank accounts, or keep them active? Cancel credit cards or keep them? Transfer money to account in destination country, or use my homeland account?
Social	Have one farewell party for all, or small parties for different groups?
The move	Take electrical appliances / furniture, or buy there? Which shipping company?

4. Now that you have identified your main decisions, the next step is information gathering.
Write down next to each task or decision the information you need to have in order to complete the task at hand or to make an informed decision.

Task / decision	Information required

5. The next step is task planning.
Use the list of tasks you have identified in Step 2, and
create a step-by-step plan for every task you have listed.
This requires you to break down your bigger tasks into
smaller steps, and then schedule them in your planner.

Use the template below to break your bigger tasks into
smaller steps. Do not forget to include, where relevant,
an information-gathering step.

Planning sheet	
Task:	

Steps	Due date
Step 1	
Step 2	
Step 3	
Step 4	
Step 5	

Congratulations! You have just created a plan for each of
your relocation tasks. Together they make your Relocation
Plan.

6. This step is about timing your plan, scheduling it in your planner, and creating daily to-do lists to follow. The most efficient way of doing this is "backward planning." In this, you start from your due dates and work back to today.

When you are working through your planner, it is useful to schedule your bigger or more complex tasks first. It is also important to be aware that some projects are dependent on completion of others and, therefore, need to be prioritized.

Once this step is complete, the tasks you scheduled for each day can be used as your daily to-do list.

7. Implementing your plan.
If you have followed the previous steps, you should have a timed plan, as well as daily to-do lists. The next step is to act on it!

It is useful to begin the implementation process as early as possible (six months in advance is optimal), and to do a little every day.

Breaking the bigger tasks into smaller chunks, then taking small action steps toward your relocation goals on a regular basis (every day/week) has two benefits. The first is that it builds your relocation "muscle" as you become used to thinking about it and working toward it. The second is that you get things done slowly and in a controlled manner, which significantly reduces the stress.

Now that your plan is ready, the list of things to be done may seem long and daunting. Where possible, consider delegating some of the tasks to other people, whether family members, friends, professionals, or hired help.

If you are still employed, try to resist the temptation to remain employed until the day you relocate, and don't agree to work overtime just before you leave. You will need to devote this time to your relocation.

Chapter 3

EFFECTIVE INFORMATION GATHERING

Information is a key element of your relocation. It is a vital component of both your decision-making process and your planning and implementation process.

Gathering information on the life that you will lead in your destination country is important to ensure that your expectations in all areas of life—employment, schooling, your finances, the social aspect, and others—are realistic.

Unrealistic expectations are one of the main causes of culture shock and relocation failure. Thus, the higher the quality of information you can gather, the better.

Surprisingly, one of the most challenging issues for many travelers, especially during the decision-making phase, is finding the right information. I have trained people who complained that they were unable to make a decision regarding their relocation simply because they could not find the information they needed. Others said that there was too much information, and that they were simply overwhelmed by it all. Funnily enough, they are both right!

There are indeed massive amounts of information available to travelers these days, much of which is provided by official authorities and accessible through the Internet. Much of this information is general, and is intended to give you a knowledge base. However, if you have a specific question, or if you require a particular piece of information, this is where it may get a little more complicated.

THE INFORMATION-GATHERING PROCESS

There are four aspects of the information-gathering process that you need to consider:

✦ Where and how to find the information required, in your language.

✦ Once you have found relevant information, how to sort it and extract what you need without being distracted by the sheer amount of material.

✦ How to handle and store the information you have gathered in an efficient way for future use.

✦ How to turn the pieces of information that you have collected into a coherent body of knowledge.

For Efficient Information Gathering . . .

✦ Identify the type of information you require.

✦ Identify sources for the information you require, and consider who or what is likely to be the best source.

✦ Contact the information provider directly.

Identifying the type of information you require is an essential step toward making your search more effective and less time consuming.

Whether you are at the decision-making phase or have already relocated, it is useful to look at the list below and think, "What type of information do I need right now to make an informed decision, or to complete the task at hand?"

Types of Information

✦ Information on processes (such as how to open a bank account).

✦ Information on a particular issue or topic (such as culture, climate, housing).

✦ Information about organizations (such as schools, health providers, banks).

✦ Information about sources of information.

Prepare a list of questions that you wish to have answered,

and search for that specific information. Stay focused, and don't spend time reading general information, articles, news, or any other matter that is not specifically discussing the points you want answered. Unfocused searching wastes time, distracts you, leads to information overload and mental fatigue, and delays the information-gathering process.

Select from the list below the sources that are likely to provide this information and contact them directly.

Sources of Information
+ Your homeland embassy in the destination country.
+ The host country embassy in your homeland.
+ Official government Web sites.
+ Books, tourist guidebooks, CDs, maps, newspapers, expatriates' newsletters, and DVDs.
+ Travel agencies and tour guides.
+ The expatriate or emigrant community in your destination country.
+ Expatriates' or immigrants' Web sites, forums, and social media sites.
+ Immigrants and returnees from your destination country residing in your homeland.
+ Relocation consultants and cross-cultural trainers.
+ Relevant charities and volunteer organizations.
+ Professionals working internationally, such as immigration lawyers, financial advisers, insurance brokers, and health professionals.

> Invest in a good tourist guidebook.
> Buy it before your move. You may not be able
> to find it in your language in your
> destination county.

INFORMATION GATHERING, STEP-BY-STEP

The previous pages reviewed some general information-gathering strategies. However, here I aim to alert you to particular aspects of the relocation journey in which misinformation or lack of information can result in adverse outcomes. Follow the notes below to create focus and order in your information-gathering process.

The Legal Aspect

Getting reliable information about legal matters is vital, both to avoid problems and to give you peace of mind.

There are several areas in which it is crucial for you to understand the law. These are: immigration and employment policies, housing, customs regulations, driving laws, and health care policies.

Immigration Laws

❑ Learn what your immigration status will be in your host country.

❑ Find out what immigration documents—passports, visas, work permits, licenses, or agreements—you are likely to be asked to present both on arrival and later on. In most countries, if you intend to stay for more than a few weeks or months, you will be required to obtain a visa, an entry permit, or a residency permit. In some countries you will be required to have just one of these, and in some, you will be required to have two or three different documents. Note that for some countries a visa is a stamp or a page in your passport, while for others it may be a certificate or an official letter. In most cases, the embassy of your destination country will issue these documents. For most countries, it is crucial to obtain these documents prior to moving.

❑ Find out the procedures that you need to follow for the required immigration documents to be issued, their cost, and the time involved.

❑ When applying for visas or residency permits you may be required to hand in your passport, meaning that you will be unable to travel abroad during the processing period. Remember to take this into account when planning your preliminary visits to your destination country.

❑ In most countries, you will be asked whether you have a criminal record, and in some you will be required to obtain a reference or certificate from the police or other authorities.

❑ You may be required to show a letter of invitation or a reference from an organization or a person in the destination country in order to obtain a visa.

❑ As you go through the legal procedures, you may be required to present some documents (such as birth or marriage certificates, or professional, employment, or educational records). Find out whether these documents need to be translated and approved by a notary.

Employment Laws

❑ Make inquiries about your family's legal employment status, and what permits you will be required to have in order to work legally in your destination country.

❑ For most countries, once you have obtained a visa or a residency permit, this will specify whether you are entitled to work there. For some other countries, however, a separate work permit is required to be able to work there legally, and it is important to obtain this prior to your move.

❑ Many professionals today—doctors, nurses, lawyers, accountants, psychologists, and others—may need to undergo tests and recertification in order to practice their profession in their destination country. Find out if this is the case regarding your profession, and, if so, the procedures you need to be aware of.

❑ If you are setting up a business abroad, it is essential to find out the relevant legal requirements and policies.

Housing

❑ Whether you will be renting or buying a property, you are likely to need certain documents for the transaction. Find out what these are, and whether you will need the help of a lawyer in these transactions.

Customs Regulations
❑ In preparation for shipping your belongings, make inquiries about the customs or import regulations that you need to comply with.

Driving
❑ If you intend to drive abroad, find out how to obtain a local (or international) driver's license.
❑ If you intend to import your car, first contact the embassy of your destination country to find out whether the car is suitable to drive there. Ask whether any modifications to the vehicle are required, and about customs and any other taxes payable. Investigate the insurance requirements in your destination country.
❑ Find out in advance what documents are required when renting, buying, or leasing a car, along with the costs involved and the insurance requirements.

Health
❑ Some countries require you to carry an international vaccination card. Find out if this is the case in your destination country and, if so, how to obtain it.
❑ Some countries require you to show that you are medically fit upon entry; if this is the case you will need a health certificate. Find out how to obtain this.
❑ If you are taking a pet with you, ensure you have the necessary information on health certificates and quarantine requirements.

Work
If you are planning to work abroad, it is worth conducting an information search on the following topics:
❑ Study the local job market in your destination country to assess the demand for your profession.
❑ Look at unemployment rates in your destination country or city, specifically in your profession.
❑ Find out which of your qualifications and credentials are recognized in your destination country.

❑ If your profession requires recertification, find out what the procedure is.

❑ Inquire what types of jobs are offered that require knowledge of your native language. Often there is a small job market in which your language is in demand.

❑ If you are considering the possibility of becoming self-employed or starting your own business, find out in advance what is involved in setting up a business presence.

❑ Inquire about typical salaries for your profession, as well as benefits and taxation.

❑ Find out how to apply for a job in your destination country, and what you need to prepare for job hunting. Find out the local conventions and timings regarding job applications, CVs, cover letters, recommendations, work portfolios, interviews, and employment exams.

❑ Find out which of your documents need to be translated into the local language, and which need to be certified by a notary.

❑ Find out whether you can take exams and job interviews in your native language.

❑ Test the job market by conducting a job search prior to your arrival. Search for job offers online in newspapers, employment Web sites, employment agencies, and on expatriate and working abroad organizations and forums.

❑ Job agencies that find work overseas are useful and can save you much time. Many organize visas, work permits, and accommodation for successful applicants.

❑ If you are not fluent in the local language, consider hiring a translator who can help you to read advertisements, communicate with potential employers, and prepare your employment documents according to the local requirements.

❑ Make inquiries about working conditions in your destination country: days and hours of employment, holidays and vacations, meals, and overtime.

❑ Take time to learn about local work practices and business etiquette (see Chapter 7).

Finances and Banking

Prior to your relocation, it is crucial to prepare financially. This involves getting accurate information and thoroughly investigating all the expenses associated with the move itself and the costs of living in the destination country.

Some points to consider

❑ Carefully assess all the costs of your move, including the shipment, farewell parties, flights, ground transportation, temporary accommodation, setting up your household abroad, and loss of income during the transition period.

❑ Investigate thoroughly the costs of day-to-day living in your new country, and measure these against the income you expect to earn.

❑ Find out what documents are required for opening a bank account.

❑ If you are leaving bank accounts open in your homeland, ensure you know how to handle your banking affairs from abroad.

Health and Safety

Although you can't anticipate every health and safety issue you may encounter when living abroad, you can decrease the chances of becoming ill and running into problems if you take the time to inform yourself about the health care system, and safety issues, in your destination country.

Some points to consider

❑ Make inquiries about the immunizations required by your destination country, and any precautionary or preventive medication that you will need to take prior to your move.

❑ Learn about the standard of local health services, so that you will know what to expect.

❑ Find out about your entitlement to health care with regard to your legal status.

❑ Consider private health insurance where available.

❏ Find out what documents you will need in order to register with local health providers or private insurance companies.

❏ Make inquiries about travel health insurance to cover you during your first months abroad.

❏ If you take regular medication or vitamins, find out whether these are available locally.

❏ Inform yourself about local crime patterns, including terrorist activity, and how to keep safe. Embassies often give briefings or issue publications to their citizens about these matters.

Education

If you are traveling with children, it is essential that you take time to acquaint yourself with the local educational system, policies, and schools.

Some points to consider

❏ Make inquiries about the schooling system, and what schools are like in terms of their academic standards, discipline, curriculum, religious education, dress code, exams, progression to the next level, and the assistance provided to newly arrived children and to children with special needs, if necessary.

❏ Find out the costs involved for both private and public education. Note that public education in some countries is not free.

❏ If there is an expatriate or an emigrant community from your homeland in your destination city, it is worth finding out which schools their children attend. Your children may find the first months of schooling less stressful if there is someone around them who can speak their language and offer support.

❏ Find out how and when to register children in schools and kindergartens, and what documents are required.

❏ Explore the availability and costs of household help, nannies, babysitters, summer camps, afternoon classes, daycare, after-school care, and sports activities for children.

Living Conditions

Many travelers don't recognize the significance of the changes they are likely to experience in their physical environment—the climate, housing, nutrition, and routines. To prepare yourself adequately for life in your new country, you will need to gather information about some of the following living conditions.

Climate and Environmental Aspects

❑ Getting used to a different climate is not only about temperature, rainfall, humidity, pollution, and hours of daylight, but also about the distinctive plants, animals, and insects that inhabit the area. It's a good idea to acquaint yourself with these aspects prior to your arrival, especially if any family members suffer from allergies.

❑ Find out also about the means that are used to deal with harsh weather conditions—what kind of heating or air-conditioning systems are used, how efficient they are, how much they cost, and what you should be aware of when renting a house and buying a car.

Housing

❑ Take some time to study the housing styles in the area where you are likely to live. Many travelers don't recognize the importance of their home to their sense of well-being, and don't take the time to familiarize themselves with the local lifestyle.

❑ Make inquiries about the typical house sizes, gardens, parking spaces, furnishings, and appliances you can expect, along with the materials and colors used, lighting, standards of tidiness and cleanliness, crowding and privacy standards, typical odors, and noise levels.

❑ Find out about utilities and what you can expect regarding service times and costs. What regulations should you be aware of? What documents will you be required to present in order to be supplied with these services?

❑ If you already know the specific area in which you are likely to live, find out what types of local services, such as banks, hospitals, and shops, there are.

❑ Familiarize yourself with typical housing costs, including rent, mortgage, government and local taxes, and utilities.

❑ If there are emigrants or expatriates from your homeland living in your destination city, find out in which areas they live.

❑ In some countries it is common to employ domestic help, and it may well be a necessity, not a luxury. Find out if this is the norm in your destination country, the costs involved, and what you need to know and consider when employing domestic help.

Food and Drink

Food and local eating habits may take some getting used to. Local food may taste different from what you are used to, or may be cooked differently, or may seem bland or heavy.

❑ During your information-gathering period, familiarize yourself with the tastes and ingredients of the local cuisine.

❑ In some countries raw fruits and vegetables need to be disinfected before they can be consumed. Find out if this is the case in your destination country.

❑ In some countries water cannot be drunk from the tap. If this is the situation in your destination country, find out how to purify water.

❑ In some countries alcohol is forbidden. Find out the regulations in your destination country.

Dress

Dress isn't only about fashion. Clothing has to be suitable for the climate, as well as socially appropriate for the culture and particular event. Additionally, it is a status symbol. It is often used to communicate a message about your power, wealth, honor, the level of formality required at an event, and your sexual availability. These vary greatly between cultures. You may find that what you wear in your homeland is simply not suitable for your host country.

❑ Before packing your clothes, check with someone in your host country about dress codes at work, in public, and for leisure and social events.

❑ It is usually a good idea to dress as the locals do, and ensure your clothing doesn't offend others.

Transportation
❑ Inform yourself about local traffic laws and how they differ from those of your homeland.
❑ If you intend to use public transportation, find out about safety issues and availability, schedules, and cost. Most tourist guidebooks are likely to have a section about transportation.

Communications and Media
❑ During your fact-finding period, and when you are on an inspection visit, explore the programs available on local TV, radio, and satellite/cable services.
❑ Find out about the availability, costs, and coverage of phone lines and cell phone services.
❑ You may want to inquire about using your cell phone from home in the destination country.
❑ You may be able to buy a cell phone suitable for your destination country in your homeland.
❑ In some places you may be able to rent or buy a cell phone at the airport. Find out what documents are required to complete these transactions.
❑ Make inquiries about Internet availability and costs, and postal services.

Culture and Language
❑ Learning about the social and cultural aspects of your intended destination is essential. This will enable you to examine the differences between your homeland and your new country, and assess whether you will fit in and feel comfortable when living there. It will also optimize your chances of settling in quickly and making new friends. In Chapter 7 you will find some guidelines on learning about the new culture, which can be used to steer yourself through your initial research.

❏ It is important to acquaint yourself not only with the routines and essentials of everyday life in the new country, but also to find out how foreigners are viewed and how you are likely to be treated by locals as regards your gender, sexual orientation, nationality, race, religion, ethnicity, or family makeup.

❏ If your language skills are poor, it is important to find out what other languages are spoken in your destination country—specifically your native language—and how this will affect your integration.

Community Life

❏ If your chosen country has few other foreign expatriates, consider whether you might feel isolated, or whether you will enjoy the experience of being the only foreigner(s) in the local community. Life can be very challenging if hardly anyone else speaks your language and the culture is radically different.

Remember that if you go to a country with a large expatriate population you will have an almost ready-made social network, there will probably be international schools that your children can attend, and you will be able to find familiar imported products.

❏ On the other hand, those living almost exclusively in large expatriate communities miss out on getting to know the locals and experiencing the native culture—often one of the most rewarding aspects of living in a different country.

❏ You and your family may be involved in some interests at home that might not be available in your new country, such as particular leisure, sports, or social activities, or religious institutions. Before your move it is worth investigating the availability or accessibility of these activities in the new environment.

THE EXPLORATORY TRIP

An exploratory trip to your destination country is a vital part of your pre-relocation fact-finding. It is highly recommended that before you move you (and your spouse) take the time to visit your destination country and the specific area where you wish to live during the early phases of your stay.

Even if you have visited before as a tourist, it is important to go again to look at things from the perspective of a resident. You are likely to notice things that you did not notice on your earlier visits.

Try to meet some people who can tell you about the country and its culture, and what you can expect as a newcomer.

Some points to consider when arranging your exploratory trip

❑ Complete the goal-setting and planning exercises in Chapter 1 prior to this trip.

❑ Collect information about the host country and its people and culture, as well as about the area where you are likely to live.

❑ If the weather in your destination country is very different from that of your homeland, consider scheduling your visit during a season that will give you a taste of the unfamiliar weather conditions.

❑ Make sure the trip won't coincide with local holidays or vacation times.

❑ Buy a good tourist guidebook.

❑ Arrange to have a relocation consultant, a veteran emigrant from your homeland, an expatriate, or an acquaintance (preferably someone who speaks your language) to show you around the areas where you plan to live, work, or study.

During Your Exploratory Trip

❑ Try to stay close to the area where you are likely to be living. If possible, avoid staying in a hotel, opting for a short let or a B&B, so that you can get a feel of what local homes look and feel like.

❑ Schedule meetings in advance with expatriates or emigrants from your homeland who can tell you about their lives, and how they differ from life in your homeland.

❑ Here are some of the points for discussion and questions you can ask them:
  • What kind of lifestyle do they have, and how does it differ from that of your homeland? What lifestyle can you expect to lead upon relocation?
  • What changed in their everyday routines for better or worse? What took some getting used to?
  • What are the main features of the host people and their culture? What aspects of the host culture have they found pleasant? Unpleasant? Surprising?
  • How long did it take them and their children to adjust?
  • What is their relationship with local people like? Do they consider themselves integrated?
  • What do they miss from home?
  • What did they wish they had known prior to their arrival?
  • What would they do in your situation?
  • Can they refer you to other sources of information and people who can help you?

❑ Try to locate someone who has achieved similar goals to those you have set, and ask them about the process you can expect to experience.

❑ Look at possible housing and find out where most emigrants and expatriates from your homeland live. Ask why they choose those particular areas, and what services are available there.

❑ Visit schools and collect information about education. Find out what schools are like in terms of discipline, curriculum, academic standards, religion, dress code, exams, progression to the next level, and assistance provided to newly arrived children. Which schools do expatriates' children attend? How do you go about registering the children for school? Also ask about household help, babysitters, summer camps, and other amenities for children.

❑ Look at local health care, recreational facilities, banking, shopping areas, and transportation services.

❑ Ask about living expenses, the income you can expect to earn in your profession, and financial aspects you may need to consider (taxes, insurance). Carefully assess both the costs of your move and the costs of day-to-day living against your projected income.

❑ Find out about employment opportunities, and ask what documentation regarding your formal training or experience you may be asked to provide, and whether these documents need to be translated.

❑ Find out about household items, furnishings, and electrical appliances.

❑ Ask about goods not available locally, which you might want to bring from home.

❑ Collect the contact details of people you meet and ask if they are willing to answer follow-up questions.

❑ Keep a journal of your trip, noting what you gleaned from each event, visit, or meeting, and take photos back to show other members of the family.

❑ Take time to enjoy the sights and places.

❑ Look both at the positive things you can look forward to and at the negative aspects.

❑ Locate people who are able and willing to assist you with information and practical help on your arrival, and can take the role of mentors—people who can act as your "carers," or "door openers," as well as information providers.

Now that you have gathered the information you require, it's time to move from planning to action, and this is what the next chapters are about.

Chapter 4

PRACTICAL PREPARATION

Once you have put your plan on paper, it's time to swing into action and begin your preparation for the move.

> For the most part, preparation involves dealing with the practical side of your move—arranging the shipment, the paperwork, the flights, and other aspects.
> It may also involve language or cross-cultural training.
> However, the most important type of preparation, and perhaps the least addressed by travellers, is psychological preparation—taking the time to reflect on your move, and comprehend the changes that are likely to occur in your life.

The trouble with the practical preparation is that engaging with the details of the move triggers the psychological preparation mechanism, forcing us to reflect on the impending changes. This often provokes a deep emotional reaction, with mixed feelings ranging from excitement, anticipation, and hope to stress, anxiety, sadness, and, at times, cold feet. When this happens, our natural instinct is to put our preparation on hold, until we feel that we are psychologically ready to deal with it. The problem with this is that it is the very actions we take that help us to develop psychological readiness and resilience, not the other way around.

In the interviews that I have conducted with travelers, I have found that those who delayed their preparation were not only creating a stressful and chaotic transition for themselves, but were also psychologically ill prepared for the challenges, and had low reserves of resilience to draw upon. Consequently, some of them experienced a "crash landing" (an eventuality that I shall address in Chapter 16).

Therefore, *do not give in to this instinct!* Make time to prepare and take action, and the sooner you start, the better. An optimal time frame is to begin your preparation six months prior to your move.

The following guidelines are designed to help you introduce order and structure into your preparation arrangements.

THE LEGAL ASPECT

Putting legal matters in order is essential. There is nothing worse than being on the wrong side of the law in a foreign country, where you cannot communicate properly, have no support system, and have no idea what the penalty might be.

Immigration: the Paperwork

❑ First, attend to your immigration documents. Apply early for all necessary documents to avoid last-minute panics.

❑ Make sure that passports, visas, work permits, and agreements are valid.

❑ Ensure that all documents that need to be translated and approved by a notary are in order.

❑ Photocopy all your documents, including passports, and keep the copies in a safe place.

❑ Take an extra set of passport photos with you.

Employment

❑ Ensure you have to hand all legal documents regarding your employment, including educational and professional certificates and contracts.

❑ If you intend to operate your own business abroad, ensure you have all that is required in terms of legal paperwork.

❑ If you will be employing other people who will also be relocating, either in your business or in your home, such as domestic help or a nanny, make sure you comply with local laws and policies.

Accommodation

❑ Ensure that all documents required for renting or buying your home are in order. Make copies of them.

❑ You may need the assistance of a lawyer in renting or buying a home. Network in advance to find one who can speak your language, and keep his or her details safely for when they are needed.

Customs

❑ If you are shipping items that require clearing through customs, ensure you have all the paperwork to hand so that you can claim your items upon arrival.

Driving

❑ Renew your driver's license in good time.

❑ If required, ensure that you have an international driver's license.

❑ Make sure you have all the necessary documents required to obtain a local driving license, rent or buy a car, release your imported car from customs, and obtain car insurance.

Health

❑ If your destination country requires you to carry an international vaccination card, ask your doctor to provide one, and keep it together with your passport.

❑ If you are taking your pet with you, ensure you comply with the policies regarding health certificates and quarantine requirements.

WORK

Before you begin your job hunt, take the following preparatory steps.

❏ Now that you have studied the local job market and assessed the demand for your profession, consider what kind of work you can realistically expect to do, given your credentials and experience.

❏ If your profession requires recertification, make sure you have with you upon arrival all the necessary exam materials, and make time to prepare for recertification.

❏ How well do you speak the local language? Unless you are fluent, take into account that you will not be competing on equal terms with local candidates. Be prepared to take jobs for which you may be overqualified.

❏ What types of jobs are offered that require knowledge of your native language? As noted above, there may be a small job market in which your language will be in demand. However, this also could mean taking a job for which you are overqualified or even changing your line of work altogether.

❏ Consider the possibility of becoming self-employed or starting your own business.

❏ Assess carefully the financial implications of not finding a job, and consider how long you can afford to be unemployed.

❏ Prepare for job-hunting by making copies of your CV and cover letter written in the local language. Where relevant, prepare a portfolio of your work.

❏ Photocopy your educational certificates.

❏ Obtain letters of recommendation and ensure you have the correct contact information of your referees.

❏ During your preparation trip (discussed on page 70), it is a good idea to purchase a local cell phone, and to have business cards with your local contact details printed and ready for your relocation. This will help you to keep in touch with potential employers.

practical preparation

❑ Begin your job search prior to your arrival. Search for job offers in online newspapers, employment Web sites, employment agencies, and on expatriate and working abroad organizations and forums.

❑ Hire a translator if you are having difficulty reading advertisements.

❑ Network! Contact family, friends, colleagues, and acquaintances in both countries, and use social media sites.

❑ When you are offered jobs it is important that you evaluate them carefully before acceptance. Be sure to have all your questions answered.

❑ If you are offered a contract, examine it carefully. Ensure that it contains all financial conditions, that you fully understand all the details, and that all the terms are acceptable to you before you sign. Find out the repercussions of breaking the contract if the job does not work out. It may be worth having a lawyer inspect the contract.

❑ Find out where the organizations you are considering working for are located. Assess the distances involved in traveling to work, and transportation means and costs.

❑ If you are being sent by your current employer, take time to visit your workplace during your preparation trip, and acquaint yourself with office staff and working conditions.

FINANCES AND BANKING

Putting your financial matters in order is essential to keep your peace of mind. The one thing that is guaranteed to trigger culture shock early in your journey is finding yourself in a foreign country with no cash!

Some points to consider

❑ Carefully assess the cost of your move and the cost of day-to-day living against your projected income.

❑ Ensure you have enough money to last you for a few months, and also put some aside to cover unplanned occurrences or changes of circumstance.

❏ Prepare and photocopy the documents that you will require for opening a bank account.

❏ It is worth leaving your current account in your homeland running for the first year or two, as well as international credit cards and savings accounts. This is simply a safety measure to protect you from any unforeseen circumstances.

❏ Arrange a way to handle your banking from abroad, and find ways to withdraw cash overseas.

❏ Decide how to handle credit card bills and any other ongoing income and expenses.

❏ Before traveling, exchange some money and, where relevant, purchase travelers' checks.

HEALTH AND SAFETY
Some points to consider

❏ Arrange a pre-departure medical examination.

❏ Ensure that you receive the required immunizations or preventive medication in time.

❏ If you take regular medication or vitamins, plan ahead to take an adequate supply with you, unless you are sure that you will be able to purchase them overseas.

❏ If you wear glasses or contact lenses, see your optician prior to departure and take a spare pair with you, as well as a copy of your prescription.

❏ Prepare a first-aid kit, and include a good medical reference book.

❏ Ensure that you have all the required documents to enable you to register with local health services as soon as you arrive.

❏ Check that your health insurance will cover you during your first months abroad until you register with local doctors and get a local health insurance plan.

❏ If raw fruits and vegetables need to be disinfected before they can be eaten in your destination country, familiarize yourself with the disinfectants and how to use them. It may be useful to bring appropriate disinfectants with you. Teach children to safeguard themselves when eating and drinking.

❏ Make sure that you, and everyone traveling with you, including children, are well informed and aware of local crime patterns, including terrorist activity, and know how to keep safe on the streets and at home. Embassies often give briefings or issue publications to their citizens about this matter, and how to protect your home while living abroad, and expatriates are likely to be well informed about this.

EDUCATION
If you are traveling with children, take time to inform them about and prepare them for their new environment.

Some points to consider
❏ Take photos of schools, and make arrangements for your children to visit the schools.
❏ Arrange to relocate before the school year begins, or during a holiday, so that your children can get used to their new home before they start school.
❏ Arrange for them to meet others of their age who go to the same school *before* they start. This will ease their adjustment to the new school.
❏ Arrange to be available during the first weeks of school.
❏ Ensure you have all the necessary documents to register your children at school. In some countries you will need to make applications months before the school year begins.
❏ Take time to explain to your children the rules and customs of their new environment: what they can expect, what teachers are likely to expect of them, and the rules they need to comply with.

HOUSING
This is an area that may require some adaptation on your part. As we have noted, the sizes of apartments, houses, gardens, and roads, the materials used, crowding and privacy standards, colors, lighting, odors, noise, furnishings and appliances, and

standards of tidiness and cleanliness are some of the aspects
that may be different from home and that may take some
getting used to.

Some points to consider

❑ Your living space overseas may be smaller than you are
used to. Be prepared to limit the amount of furniture,
appliances, and other items you take with you when
relocating. When visiting homes during your preparation
trip, take a tape measure to get an accurate measurement
of room sizes.

❑ Ensure that any electrical appliances you intend to take
with you are suitable, and in good condition. Be aware
that you may not be able to get them serviced or find
replacement parts abroad.

❑ If there is an expatriate or emigrant community in your
target area, you will need to decide whether you wish to
live near your countrymen or not. It is often a good idea to
live in close proximity to your countrymen at least during
the first years of your relocation. This will enable you to
enjoy the practical and emotional support you and your
family may need during the first stages of your adaptation.
This is discussed in more detail in Chapter 5.

❑ If you are traveling with children who don't speak the local
language, it may be useful to take with you some DVDs
and a DVD player or laptop computer with some films
and games in their own language.

VACATIONS, GOING HOME, AND FAMILY VISITS
This may seem like an irrelevant issue to deal with during
the preparation phase, but it is a good idea to plan your first
vacations ahead and take time to think about visiting your
home and family during the first year of your relocation.
Share your plans with family members and friends at home.
This is particularly important if you are leaving behind elderly
relatives, or youngsters who will be starting boarding school
or college in your homeland.

Planning ahead and scheduling mutual visits will give both you and them something to look forward to, and will create a sense of continuity in your relationships. However, if you are inviting relatives over, ensure that they are those you enjoy spending time with, and who will support you. The last thing you need during your initial period abroad is a demanding visitor whose company you find unpleasant.

Consider the responsibilities that you will continue to have in your original country after you have moved. A common example is that of voting. If you are required to vote after your relocation, contact the relevant electoral administration offices and request to be registered as an overseas voter in order to have the appropriate forms sent out to you.

THE PREPARATION TRIP

A preparation trip to your destination country is a vital part of the relocation preparation. The preparation trip is often conducted a few weeks before the relocation day, and is very different from the exploratory trip described on page 59. This is because it is focused on getting things done, and on bringing some of the settling-in arrangements to completion, as well as collecting specific and detailed information that will enable you to find your feet more quickly after your arrival. The aim of the preparation trip is to enable you and your family to have a softer and more comfortable landing.

The following points and many others can be dealt with after your move, but it is strongly recommended that you attempt to address and arrange as much as possible beforehand. The more you are able to arrange before your move, the easier and more relaxed your initial settling-in period is likely to be.

Some points to consider before your preparation trip

❑ Complete the planning exercise in Chapter 2.
❑ Make a list of everything that you want to arrange during your trip (such as, open a bank account, rent a house, register children for school, locate a mentor—see

Chapter 5). Ensure that your list is realistic in terms of timing, taking into account that things may take longer than expected.
❑ Make sure you know or find out in advance about how these things are done, and which documents are required to complete each item on your list.
❑ Make sure that your trip does not coincide with local holidays or vacation times.
❑ Where necessary, schedule meetings in advance with schools, employers, lawyers, and others.
❑ Plan to have a cell phone and a laptop computer with you, or to rent or buy a local cell phone.
❑ If you will be using public transportation, ensure you have information about the available services, costs, and schedules.
❑ Arrange for a realtor or relocation consultant to show you around the areas where you plan to live, work, or study, and assist you with information and guidance.
❑ Arrange to stay close to the area where you are likely to live.
❑ Schedule meetings in advance with expatriates or emigrants from your homeland who can offer you advice and support. Ask them to refer you to other sources of information and people who can help you and your family when you arrive.

During your preparation trip
❑ Look at possible housing, and local facilities such as schools, health care, recreational facilities, banking, shopping areas, and transportation services.
❑ Shop locally to acquaint yourself with the stores and products.
❑ If you are renting a place, make a list or take photos of the appliances and furnishings, and note what is missing and what you should bring with you.
❑ Inquire about goods not available locally and note what you might wish to bring from home.
❑ Ask about services such as telephone, cable, Internet, gas, electricity, and water services and, where possible, make arrangements for their supply.

❑ If you are seeking work, look at possible employment opportunities. Be sure to have with you all the necessary documents.

❑ Look at local schools and kindergartens, and, where possible, register your children at local schools. Ask about household help, babysitters, and nannies.

❑ Find a relocation consultant or a mentor.

SMALL DETAILS THAT MAKE ALL THE DIFFERENCE

One of the features of the early stages of relocation is "learning to do without"—managing without little things that "they don't have," "we can't get," or "we can't do" in the destination country. These things may be a particular food or drink, an activity or a service, an appliance, a certain type of entertainment or fashion. To avoid the frustration and nuisance of this, you can take the following steps.

❑ List these items. What are your favorite foods, drinks, hobbies, or activities that you may wish to continue enjoying abroad?

❑ Find out if these are available in your destination country.

❑ If they are not available, arrange in advance to address these issues. You can find substitutes, bring some items with you, or arrange to have them sent to you on a regular basis.

❑ When you are choosing where to live, consider living near those areas where you can easily gain access to your preferred hobbies or sports.

The key to resolving these issues is to be aware of them. Being aware helps you to cope, because now that you expect them you can either adopt a different attitude toward these things and accept doing without them, or be more proactive and attempt to get them. The outcome is that you don't become annoyed or upset about it. Awareness indeed makes us more resilient.

Now that the practical details of your preparation are all in order, it's time to create a support network for you and your family—and this is what the next chapter is about.

Chapter 5

ESTABLISHING A SUPPORT SYSTEM

In your homeland you probably have many people to whom you can turn for all kinds of advice, support, or help: family, friends, neighbors, the local community, your doctor, religious organizations, and others.

> Once you have relocated, you will need to rebuild your support network—and the sooner the better!

Having a support system in the destination country can significantly lessen the difficulties of the settling-in period, so it is enormously helpful to start setting it up before your arrival.

Don't wait until you relocate to search for and generate a support network. You will need much support during those crucial first days of arrival and, therefore, the earlier you begin to network and establish relationships, the better.

> It is most likely that your initial connections
> will be with your fellow countrymen,
> be they expatiates or emigrants from your homeland,
> currently residing in your destination country.

Members of your compatriot community can be a great source of help. They know what you are going through and can sympathize and provide practical and emotional support.

Start contacting them several months before you relocate. The easiest ways to find your fellow countrymen are by going through your homeland's embassy and community organizations in your destination country, expatriates' or emigrants' Web sites and forums, social media sites, and relocation consultants.

Immigrants and returnees from your destination country living in your homeland and professionals working internationally—such as immigration lawyers, financial advisors, insurance brokers, and health professionals—can also be a great link to people living in your destination country.

HIRING A RELOCATION CONSULTANT

Relocation companies or consultants are service providers who assist people in moving internationally. They vary greatly in size and in the type and scope of the services they offer.

Some companies focus on relocating individuals and families, while others specialize in corporate relocation.

Larger companies are capable of providing support both before and after relocation, whereas smaller companies are more focused on the post-relocation period. Some offer practical help and will organize and do some of the relocation tasks for you, while others mainly offer advice and information.

The service may include assistance with shipping, including shipping of vehicles, arranging visas and work permits, flights, temporary accommodation, car rental or ground transportation, and a cell phone. It may also include help with arrangements for animals that need to be quarantined.

Larger companies may have a consultant who speaks your language; others may not, but may provide an interpreter if necessary. Some companies offer cross-cultural and language training in addition to logistics.

Post-relocation assistance is likely to include welcoming you at the airport and driving you to your accommodation, buying essential groceries for you, and taking you around to acquaint you with the city and relevant places. They may help you to fill out official forms as required, and set up utilities. They may assist you with shopping, banking, health services, and the like, supply job leads, and help with registering children for schools.

A corporate relocation service generally undertakes the transportation of equipment, files, and other property from the old premises to the new, and often provides assistance in fitting out the new office, including connecting utilities, setting up computer networks and workstations, and other essentials such as putting up shelves.

A corporate relocation company may also help employees with relocation arrangements as well as provide training.

Ask your relocation consultant to . . .

✦ Meet you at the airport.
✦ Arrange a car rental for you, or drive you to your accommodation.
✦ Arrange for you to have a cell phone upon arrival.
✦ Check on your accommodation before you arrive and make sure everything is in working order.
✦ Shop for basic foods and necessities for the first few days.
✦ Be available during the first two weeks to show you around.
✦ Provide information you may require upon arrival.
✦ Give you a city tour and help you get acquainted with relevant areas and facilities.
✦ Take you shopping and help you take care of other arrangements, such as banking and registering children for school.
✦ Provide assistance and preparation for job hunting.
✦ Help you release your shipment from customs.
✦ Act as an interpreter or translator when needed.
✦ Link you to professionals where necessary, such as doctors, lawyers, and language teachers.
✦ Connect you to local networks and organizations.

Indeed, relocation services can provide invaluable support to newcomers, and I highly recommend using such services where they are available to ensure that your move goes as smoothly and as pleasantly as possible. They can make a huge difference to your transition, and are likely to prove one of the best financial investments you can make.

Look for a company with branches in both your homeland and your destination country, and find out what services it offers. A good place to start looking for relocation services is on the Internet, but it is also worth asking your embassy in the destination country, and expatriates and emigrants from your homeland may be able to help you locate such a service.

Charges vary, based on the types of services required for the move. Many companies offer several basic packages to choose from, and can add extra services to meet the customer's specific needs.

To work effectively with a relocation consultant, arrange for him or her to be with you for most of your preparation trip, and then during the first weeks after your arrival. List your immediate requirements and the type of help you may need. Make sure you are both clear about the nature and scope of the help and support to be provided. After the first two weeks of your relocation, you may need to hire your consultant for only a few hours or a day or two a week.

If you can't find a relocation company or consultant, consider employing a local person who has knowledge of the area, such as a realtor or a rental car driver, to assist you when you arrive.

FINDING A MENTOR

One of the most productive ways to alleviate some of the challenges of relocation is to find at least one friendly person who will act as your source of emotional support, cultural learning, and social grounding during your first months abroad. Such people are often referred to as mentors, or sponsors. Newcomers who have such a person to turn to make their transition more comfortably than those who do not.

Your mentor can provide a warm welcome, give you useful information, get things for you, help you get settled, connect you socially to other people and act as a "door opener," offer companionship and emotional support when you need it, and, importantly, can be your cultural informant—a source of knowledge on your new country and its culture. Mentors often turn into good friends, and in many cases the relationship lasts for years.

The Ideal Mentor Should Be . . .
- ✦ A person from your homeland who relocated a few years before you. Don't opt for someone with less than two years' experience of the country.
- ✦ In the same age group, with a similar family situation.
- ✦ Someone preferably living reasonably near you.
- ✦ Willing and able to devote time to help you, especially during your first weeks.
- ✦ Importantly, your mentor should be someone who is positive, caring, patient, and knowledgeable.

Your mentor may be your relocation consultant, but I have found that this is rare. Most mentors are not paid for their assistance, and this may be why relocation consultants do not take on this role.

Mentors are often family members, friends, colleagues, acquaintances, or, indeed, friends of friends. Thus, it is essential that you take the time to establish a comfortable relationship with them prior to your arrival. Despite the fact that mentors are not paid, communicate with them ahead of time and ensure that you and they are clear about the nature of the help and support they will be providing, and consider ways to acknowledge and reward their help, perhaps by bringing them a gift from your country, or inviting them out.

If you and your spouse will be arriving separately, find mentors for each of you. *Do not* rely on your spouse to be your mentor! He or she is likely to be tied up at work and figuring out challenges there, and may not have the time, patience, or experience to guide you through the process.

So, how can you find mentors? The best way is through the expatriate or immmigrant community in your destination country. Expatriates' or immigrants' Web sites and forums, social media sites, community organizations in your destination country, and relocation consultants could also be a great source of help in your search. However, surprisingly, many of the best networks are formed through returnees in your homeland (although finding them may be a bit more tricky). Try networking among your family and friends to find returnees, as well as searching on Internet forums and social media sites.

Ask Your Mentor To . . .
+ Meet you at the airport, or on the day of your arrival.
+ Be available during the first weeks to support you and show you around.
+ Take you shopping and acquaint you with other facilities and services offered in your residential area.
+ Lend you things you may need.
+ Provide information upon your arrival about schools, shops, and services.
+ Help you find doctors, lawyers, household help, babysitters, and afternoon classes.
+ Spend time with you and your family.
+ Go out with you or invite you to their homes during the first weeks.
+ Connect you to other people and families with similar interests.
+ Celebrate a festival or special occasion with you.
+ Help you prepare for your meetings with local people.
+ Help you learn about the local culture.

In this part, you have built a solid foundation for your move by addressing the practical aspects and establishing the all-important support system. The following chapters focus on the cross-cultural aspect of your journy, and offer you essential srategies for pre-location language and cultural learning.

Chapter 6

CULTURE MATTERS!

Anthropologists, sociologists, and psychologists alike have long attempted to define what culture is, and, importantly, why moving across cultures is so taxing and why it causes culture shock. The following chapters aim to address these questions, beginning with a definition of culture, followed by a review of the cross-cultural adaptation process, and ending with a suggested framework for pre-relocation cross-cultural learning.

> ### *WHAT IS CULTURE?*
> Culture is a shared way of life. Culture includes language and communication, as well as the norms, beliefs, values, habits, customs, and routines that a group of people share.
> *Professor Clifford Geertz (1973, paraphrased)*

Culture is the sum of the collective choices that a group of people or a society has made over the years about how to live, work, communicate, celebrate, educate, learn, and relate to one another, and manage many other details of life. In time, these choices take the shape of unwritten rules or norms of behavior.

Our culture is intertwined within the routines, habits, customs, and traditions that we follow; it is embedded in the values and beliefs that we accept as right and true; and it is revealed through the standards by which we evaluate and make judgments about people and events.

> ### *CULTURE HAS THREE COMPONENTS*
> The first is language, and, more so, communication.
> The second is the concrete or practical aspect of life:
> the behavioral norms, routines, habits, and customs.
> The third incorporates the symbolic aspects of life:
> the values, attitudes, beliefs, categorizations, and
> definitions that a group of people share.

LANGUAGE AND COMMUNICATION

These are some of the details of communication that require
re-learning on international relocation:

+ Standard language and specific cultural meanings of
  words, terms, idioms, and slang.
+ Applying different registers—how to speak to children,
  adults, people in authority.
+ Norms of communication, such as speaking, listening,
  public speaking, interviewing, singing.
+ Salutations and greetings.
+ Suitable and unsuitable subjects for discussion,
  according to the occasion and the company, and
  taboo subjects.
+ How people are expected to behave—formally,
  politely, emotionally.
+ What is funny and what is not.
+ Accent, volume, pitch, and tone.
+ How people express opinions, criticize, and give praise.
+ Body language and gestures.
+ Written material, letters, and e-mails: forms of address,
  styles, presentation, and structure.
+ Conflicts and how to resolve them.

NORMS, ROUTINES, HABITS, AND CUSTOMS

These are some of the cultural norms, routines, habits, and
customs that require re-learning on relocation:

+ Etiquette: the expected appropriate behavior in
  different situations.

✦ Dress codes.
✦ Physical distance and body contact. Rules regarding touching, hugs, and kisses.
✦ General standard of living.
✦ Cleanliness of people and places.
✦ Hosting and visiting practices.
✦ Common recreation and leisure activities.
✦ Eating practices.
✦ Timing and routines. How people treat time. The general pace of life. Punctuality.
✦ The consumption of media.
✦ Sleeping practices.
✦ Status symbols.
✦ Fashions in clothing, decorating, art.
✦ Religious customs, holidays, and celebrations.

BELIEFS AND VALUES

These are some of the beliefs and values of a culture that require re-learning upon international relocation:

✦ The status and roles of people or groups in society: men, women, immigrants, the elderly, children.
✦ Ideas about aspects of life such as work, love, leisure, marriage, family, parenting, education, money, aging, and religion.
✦ The boundaries between private and public.
✦ The meaning of group affiliations such as citizenship, friendship, family, religion, race, ethnicity.
✦ Ideas about authority, discipline, and rules.
✦ How success, achievement, and winning are perceived.
✦ How people treat and react to change.
✦ Superstitions.

Cultures are living, dynamic entities that constantly change and develop. Culture is rooted in the history, geography, climate, and religion of a nation, and is influenced by political and economic factors, by development in areas such as health, education, technology, transport, and communication, and by neighboring cultures.

> Culture shapes how we dress, speak, and act, but, more importantly, it structures our way of thinking.

Culture provides us with a mental framework that determines what we perceive and what we are unable to discern, or are inclined to ignore. It also provides categories and definitions for organizing our perceptions and a set of beliefs, values, and standards that orient our thinking about ourselves, about others, and about life in general.

Our beliefs and values, some of which we are likely to be unaware of, determine how we assess and react to events, what we consider to be normal or abnormal, good or bad, true or false, ugly or beautiful, what behaviors we accept and those that we instinctively want to reject. These cultural beliefs are built into our outlook on the world, providing a reference point for understanding what we observe, and a guide for how to act.

> Culture is a group world view, a way of thinking and organizing the world that a particular society or group has created over time.

Each of us internalizes this framework, and we habitually use it as a lens through which to perceive and interpret life, to make sense of ourselves and of others, and of our experience of the world. Through this lens, we selectively perceive things; we organize what we observe in a particular way; and we interpret and make judgments about these things.

Culture is a group characteristic, not just a national feature. We are all influenced by the national culture in which we live, and particularly the culture in which we grew up. However,

other groups to which we belong also influence our cultural
outlook and add cultural layers. Gender, religion, profession,
racial, ethnic, or religious groups, and, especially, class, all
affect how we behave and how we see the world.

> Culture shapes our identity, touching and
> imprinting our psyche at the deepest level.

Our identities are formed through our affiliations and our
sense of belonging to particular societies or groups.

Our cultural framework is learned, not inherent. At birth,
we are not culturally American or Italian. As we grow up, we
are socialized into our country's culture; we observe, we are
taught, and we emulate the details of the shared way of life
that makes up our culture, and we unconsciously adopt these
guidelines as being the "normal" or the "right" way to live,
and the "proper" way to do things. We also internalize what it
means to be Australian, German, or Spanish, and we learn to
think and behave in certain ways, and not in others.

> Despite its centrality in our lives, we are often blind to
> elements of our own culture. For most of us, culture is
> largely unconscious; it is our "natural" way of being, and
> our "default mechanism." We take it for granted.

We can easily see how powerful culture is. The patterns
developed within a society or group over generations enable
its members to generate shared meanings very quickly from
the flood of daily events and occurrences. Culture makes us
feel more secure, since it creates order and predictability in
many areas of our lives, thus freeing us to be more inventive
in other areas.

Our culture directs, grounds, supports, and frames our
lives, and because it is so deeply entrenched in our psyche it

is difficult to change. We are, in many ways, prisoners of our own cultures, and without it, we are in free fall.

This is why the culture-shock phenomenon occurs and why cross-cultural exposure is, for many people, such a taxing experience.

CULTURE IS LIKE AN ICEBERG

Culture is often illustrated as an iceberg. The tip of the iceberg is easy to see: it includes the overt features of a culture—the dress, language, customs, traditions, celebrations, and some dos and don'ts. The major part of the iceberg, though, is concealed below the surface, and consists of the covert features of the culture—the values, attitudes, norms, experiences, and the thinking patterns that characterize that culture.

Venturing into an alien culture without sufficient knowledge can be as dangerous as a ship sailing through freezing waters without navigation devices, hoping to steer clear of icebergs.

The difference is that when a ship bumps into an iceberg the crew will know immediately and recognize what has happened, while unsuspecting travelers may not realize that they have bumped into a cultural iceberg. They will, however, feel the impact.

> When we enter a new culture, we lose our compass. A foreign culture is like a secret code: until we are able to unlock the code, little of what we see or experience will make much sense.

Furthermore, it is not until we are confronted with another culture that we begin to notice the features of our own culture. As our awareness grows, we recognize how irrelevant our own mindsets, habits, and customs may be in the new place.

It is these two events that occur upon relocation—the need to learn the countless minute and obscure details that make up another culture, and the understanding that we may need to unlearn much of what we know, things that are very much a part of who we are—that trigger the culture-shock experience.

However, these occasions also present a tremendous opportunity to grow: to step beyond our comfort zones; to broaden our thinking, behavior, and identities; to become more sensitive, more aware, and more tolerant of ourselves and others; and to improve our analytic skills. It is an experience of development and growth.

Chapter 7

CROSS-CULTURAL LEARNING

> If there is one thing that everyone
> who lives and works abroad has to get right,
> this is it: they must be able to get along
> with the local people.

It doesn't matter in what capacity you relocate, what goals you set, and what responsibilities you will assume—it is difficult to imagine how you can succeed if you don't interact effectively with the locals.

Yet, as I have seen in my line of work, many newcomers, including expats, do not and cannot. The reason is, in most cases, an inability to communicate in the local language and insufficient knowledge of the local culture. My advice, therefore, is simple, and perhaps seems trivial: take time to learn as much as possible of the local language and culture before you relocate.

Many people believe that it will be easier and quicker to learn a new language and culture when they are immersed in that environment. However, taking time to learn these aspects in the comfort of your own homeland, without having your knowledge tested in everyday life, will give you peace of mind during the initial period. It will enable you to move around and engage with local people with a confidence that you might not otherwise have.

Even if you have visited the country before as a tourist, take time to enhance your knowledge. There is a huge difference between taking a brief vacation and settling in as a resident, and while locals may treat a bemused tourist with good humor, they are unlikely to treat your mistakes so lightly.

Research on expatriates has shown that those who undertake some kind of cross-cultural learning, whether through formal training or private study, are much more successful in their overseas assignments than those who do not. Furthermore, insufficient cultural learning is often cited as the primary cause of relocation failure. Other costs of cultural ignorance can be social embarrassment, legal trouble, and even physical danger. It is, therefore, essential to learn as much as possible of the local language and the basic aspects of the culture before your move, and to continue after your arrival.

LANGUAGE LEARNING

"Why should we study the language before relocation?" Trainees often ask me this question, and then add their own answer: "Surely we'll pick up the language much faster and much more productively when we are immersed in it, and when circumstances simply force us to learn it!"

This, as it stands, is perfectly true. Total immersion is the best way to learn a language. However, there is also a high cost if there has been no previous study: the stress of being unable to communicate during the settling-in period; the loss of confidence; miscommunications, which can cause an array of unpleasant or even disastrous errors, delays to your plans, and, of course, the resulting culture-shock depression.

By studying the language prior to your move, you can remove the most challenging and confusing factor involved in your relocation. Every small achievement in the local language will boost your confidence and morale, while the inability to read the label on a cleaning solution, order a meal in a restaurant, or to ask a bus driver a question is likely to have a demoralizing effect. Learning the local language can make a huge difference to your settling-in experience and long-term adaptation. It can also alleviate two of the main difficulties affecting newcomers: change overload and loss of confidence (discussed in Chapter 16).

Being plunged into a foreign environment without knowing a word of the language is like regressing to the level of a newborn baby. You won't be able to understand or make sense of what's going on around you, or to convey your needs. You are likely to be more isolated and to have to confine your movements to your compatriots' circles, as well as rely on others to help you and get things done for you.

If you are planning to work or look for a job immediately on arrival, then knowing at least some of the language is an absolute must. The more proficient you are on arrival, the more self-sufficient and effective you are likely to be.

The Benefits of Pre-Relocation Language Learning
Language skills, even limited ones, can:
- Open doors for you.
- Make it possible for you to network and interact with local people.
- Enable you to function more effectively in your everyday life.
- Facilitate the process of exploring your area and the facilities available around it.
- Help you gain a better understanding of the host culture.
- Speed your adjustment.
- Improve the quality and reduce the stresses of your settling-in period.
- Elevate your confidence.
- Lessen the symptoms of culture shock.

Bear in mind that learning another language doesn't mean that you have to become fluent. Don't feel you have to wait to relocate until you have become a proficient speaker and can conduct yourself like a local person. This is not a realistic expectation. You need to know enough to function, communicate, and be comfortable in the new environment. Having an elementary or intermediate level when you arrive is better than being speechless.

Language-Training Options
- ✦ Academic courses provided by universities or adult education institutes.
- ✦ Language classes.
- ✦ A private teacher or tutor.
- ✦ Live Internet tutoring.
- ✦ Independent study (using DVDs, CDs, books, or interactive Internet sites).

It is worth considering all the options before choosing the one most suitable for you. Sometimes a combination of methods is appropriate.

Language training is vital for adults and children both before and after the move. Beginners need, on average, two years of continuous training, including three hours a week of focused study, plus exercises, to make real progress. With less than that, you will achieve little more than review what you have done before.

Note that not all expatriate companies provide the accompanying spouse with adequate language training. However, it is often the spouse who is in the front line—the person who has to speak to the local people when shopping, banking, or traveling. The spouse may be the one dealing with teachers, tutors, repair personnel, babysitters, salespeople, callers, and neighbors. A spouse with language abilities will carry out these tasks more effectively and will feel less frustrated and isolated than one without.

> Learning a language is like mastering other skills.
> Talent helps, but the main requirements are
> time, effort, and practice, and, importantly,
> the willingness to make mistakes.

The bad news is that you will make mistakes, and at times there will be misunderstandings, but that's the only way to learn. The good news is that the first hundred words are the hardest but the most important, and that learning does become easier with time and practice.

> In cross-cultural communication, it is not just what you say that matters, but also how you say it. This is where your knowledge of the norms of communication can be crucial. When learning the language, attempt to grasp the "how," as well as the "what."

LEARNING A NEW CULTURE

The reality of today's global marketplace requires companies to relocate staff to foreign locations in order to establish and operate a business presence abroad. The executives and professional staff sent to man foreign operations are usually chosen for their skills and accomplishments within their native country. However, in a cross-cultural environment their skills may become defunct.

Developing global cultural competency is one of the most challenging aspects of working internationally. Managing the myriad work and management styles that companies face across geographies, businesses, functions, and projects can be daunting. What is effective in one culture may well be ineffective, or even inappropriate, in others.

It is estimated that more than a third of all international ventures fail within two or three years. The reasons most often given are *cultural shortsightedness* and *lack of cultural competency*: the inability of employees to work effectively with a multicultural team, inability to adapt, spouse dissatisfaction, and poor job performance resulting from culture-shock depression.

A relocating manager may find it hard to create a rapport with his or her new colleagues. Then negativity starts to creep in, motivation and patience are lost, and the work environment becomes contaminated with stress, anger, and resentment. In addition, if a spouse or children are having a difficult time adjusting to the new culture, the pressure increases.

Maximizing the chances of an employee's success in a foreign location is a critical business priority. If proper training is not offered to prepare, train, and coach the employee and the family, the whole experience can turn sour and fail. This costs the company time, effort, and money, and results in a demotivated workforce, damaged reputation, and severed relationships with clients or partners.

Relocation preparation and cross-cultural training can reduce the chances of relocation failure. Cross-cultural training equips employees with essential cultural knowledge, enabling them to understand the culture of their destination and function successfully in the new environment. Relocation training helps employees and their families to deal with the changes that their relocation will introduce into their lives.

The Benefits of Relocation and Cross-Cultural Training

These forms of training . . .

✦ Prepare travelers mentally for their move.
✦ Remove some of the unknowns.
✦ Increase self-awareness and cross-cultural understanding.
✦ Provide opportunities for questions to be answered and anxieties to be addressed in a supportive environment.
✦ Motivate and excite.
✦ Reduce stress and provide coping strategies.
✦ Ease the settling-in process.
✦ Increase self-confidence and peace of mind.
✦ Help newcomers to make a favorable impression on local people.
✦ Reduce the chances of relocation failure.
✦ Reduce the occurrence of intercultural clashes.
✦ Help to beat the impact of culture shock.

There are several ways to acquaint yourself with a new culture. Cross-cultural training in the form of courses or seminars are probably the most efficient form of preparation for relocation.

If formal training is not available to you, the best alternative would be to hire a relocation consultant. Another popular method of cultural learning is self-learning.

How To Learn About a New Culture

✦ Take a cross-cultural training course.
✦ Hire a cross-cultural consultant.
✦ Take a self-taught cross-cultural training program, available in books, DVDs, or on the Internet.
✦ Specific knowledge can be acquired through books (such as the *Culture Smart!* series—see page 236), international business guides, tourist guidebooks, DVDs, and Internet sources.
✦ Seek opportunities to talk to immigrants, expatriates, or returnees from your host country living in your homeland.
✦ Look at expatriate and international business magazines and Web sites.
✦ Read some of the local literature, such as novels or magazines.
✦ Children's books are a great source of information about the customs, traditions, and norms of your host culture.
✦ Seek sensory impressions: listen to music and spoken language, watch local TV shows or films, sample the food, and look at photos and typical artefacts.
✦ Read books and articles about common cultural differences between cultures.
✦ Acquaint yourself with your own homeland's cultural features.

By definition, cross-cultural awareness means not only becoming culturally fluent in other cultures, but also having a solid understanding of your own culture. Therefore, take time to study and reflect on this. Once you recognize how your own thought patterns, behaviors, values, attitudes, and expectations have been shaped by your own culture, you will be in a better position to perceive events and interpret situations from a different point of view.

> It is easier to learn the features of a new culture
> by comparing it to the one you know well:
> the culture of your homeland.

While you are in the preparation phase, assess how different the two cultures are, and in which aspects they differ most. The exercise at the end of this chapter will guide you through this process.

Consider which areas you may find challenging. Awareness of these will render you more resilient.

In your new country you are likely to meet people who don't know much about your homeland, and it is therefore important for you to be able to talk knowledgeably about current affairs and other aspects of your country.

Types of Relocation Preparation and Cross-Cultural Training Programs

✦ General cross-cultural awareness training.
✦ Culture- or country-specific training.
✦ Relocation preparation.
✦ Language training.

General Cross-Cultural Awareness Training

This type of training deals with the manifestations of culture in life, and particularly in the workplace. Its main purpose is to evaluate and constructively tackle the challenges that cross-cultural differences present. This type of training provides participants with a better understanding of their own cultural dispositions, and of the role of culture when interacting with people from other backgrounds.

Companies that offer cross-cultural awareness courses may offer modules on such subjects as:

+ The general principles of culture.
+ Comparing and contrasting cultures.
+ How to learn about another culture.
+ Cross-cultural management.
+ Leading and working with virtual teams.
+ Understanding communication differences across cultures.
+ Negotiating across cultures.
+ Cultural diversity training.

Country-Specific Training

Country-specific training is aimed at individuals preparing for international relocation, as well as staff members who regularly visit a foreign country or frequently interact with overseas clients or colleagues.

This type of training provides information on important aspects of living and working in a specific country and culture, and therefore focuses on areas such as the country's or region's profile—geography, history, social structure, values and norms—current affairs, the business environment, business etiquette and protocol, and cross-cultural communication. This equips participants with key skills to help them build successful relationships. It also often includes language training.

Country-specific training often includes modules such as:

+ Introduction to the country, its history, politics, and culture.
+ Cultural norms, values, customs, and etiquette.
+ Work ethics.
+ Hierarchy, management, and leadership styles.
+ Building relationships, networking, meetings.
+ Sales practices, negotiations, presentations.
+ Decision making.
+ Problem solving.
+ Interpersonal communication, conversation topics, and conflict resolution.
+ Food and drink norms.
+ Gift-giving protocols.
+ Time and punctuality.

Relocation Training

Relocation preparation—which covers much of the same ground as this book—is often offered in addition to culture-specific training, with the aim of preparing travelers for the practical as well as the emotional aspects of their relocation journey.

This type of training is often offered to expatriates and their spouses and sometimes to children. It provides strategies for effectively handling their own and their family's adjustment process, including advice about moving abroad with children and tips and information for the expatriate spouse.

Typical relocation training modules are likely to include:

+ A general review of the relocation journey.
+ Change management strategies.
+ Relocation planning.
+ Information gathering.
+ Preparation for the move.
+ Preparation for the transition period: the shipping, farewell stage, and the relocation day.
+ Guidelines and tools on how to adapt and deal with cultural differences.
+ Guidance on how to cope with culture shock.

Some companies also offer repatriation preparation training, which is designed to address the reentry issues that homecoming individuals or families may face.

Language Training

Language courses that are offered to expatriates and other travelers are often much wider in scope than language courses that are academic in nature.

These language courses often include:

+ Communication norms.
+ Local vernacular or slang.
+ Communication protocols.
+ Forms of address, greetings, and introductions.
+ Typical conversation topics.

✦ Written and online communication.
✦ Conflict resolution mechanisms.
✦ Accent training.
✦ Personal space, body language, gestures, silences, pace, and tone.

All types of cross-cultural training are usually administered by cross-cultural specialists with a knowledge of living and working in the target country and experience of relocation.

THE CORE DIMENSIONS OF CULTURE
Discussing culture in the abstract can be frustrating. It may seem that understanding broad concepts may not be very useful to someone who will soon be facing the task of learning an infinite amount of small details about a specific culture. However, an understanding of the broad characteristics of cultures is as important and as useful as culture-specific training.

Understanding how cultures work, why culture matters, and the logic behind cultural practices and behaviors will go a long way in helping you adjust to your new life.

The best approach to cross-cultural learning can often be to begin your learning with the more general concepts of culture, and then move on to local, culture-specific learning.

The following notes to guide you through your initial cultural learning cover both general and specific types of training.

Essential General Cultural Knowledge
A quick and efficient way to acquaint yourself with your host culture is to apply Professor Geert Hofstede's cultural dimensions model, set out on the next page. To assess the cultural differences between your home and your host culture, complete the exercise on page 101.

> ### THE FIVE DIMENSIONS OF CULTURE
> ✦ Power distance: the relationship between individuals
>   where hierarchy exists.
> ✦ Individualism versus collectivism: the relationship
>   between individuals and groups in societies.
> ✦ Masculinity versus femininity: achievement versus
>   care orientation.
> ✦ Weak versus strong uncertainty avoidance: how
>   change and uncertainty are approached.
> ✦ Long- versus short-term orientation: the ways in
>   which time is perceived.

Power Distance

This dimension describes the relationship between individuals where hierarchy exists—parents and children, teachers and students, manager and employees, and others.

On one side of the axis we see cultures that are more hierarchical in nature, such as Iran, Turkey, Thailand, Germany, and China. These countries have a large power distance. In these cultures, might is right, power is good, less powerful people are dependent on those in charge, centralization is popular, children and subordinates are given directions and need to respect authority. The less powerful accept power relations that are autocratic or paternalistic. Subordinates acknowledge the power of others based on their formal, hierarchical positions. Relationships and speech style are relatively formal.

On the other side of the axis are equality-oriented cultures, such as the USA, Denmark, New Zealand, and Australia, where there is a small power distance between people. In these societies, people expect and accept power relations that are more consultative or democratic. Thus inequalities, privileges, and status symbols are minimized. Relationships between those in positions of power and those in lower positions are seen as interdependent. People relate to one another more as equals, regardless of formal positions. Decentralization is popular; children and subordinates expect to be consulted.

Anybody can take the lead. Relationships and speech style are relatively informal.

Individualism Versus Collectivism
This dimension describes the relationship between individuals and groups in societies, and how it varies in different societies.

On one side of the axis, we see cultures that are individualistic, such as the USA and the UK, where individuals are more important than groups, and tasks are more important than relationships. People are expected to be different, to have different opinions about things, to do their own things, to develop and display their individual personalities, and to choose their own affiliations. Self-interest and self-respect are valued. Relationships are often contractual, and people measure each other in terms of how useful they are. Communication is explicit, and you will notice in these cultures that the word "I" is used a lot.

On the other side are collectivistic cultures, such as South Korea, Singapore, and India. Here the group is more important than the individual, and people are expected to sacrifice their own resources, time, goals, and sometimes even their lives for the collective—such as the group, nation, or community. Belonging to groups and organizations is important, and people are defined and act mostly as members of long-term groups, such as their family, village, clan, religious group, age group, town, or profession, among others. Relationships are, therefore, more important than tasks, and people attempt to maintain harmony at all times. Obligation, loyalty, duty, and honor are important. Communication is imprecise and implicit, assuming that people who are members of the group understand what is being implied without the need for words. The most commonly used word is "we."

Masculinity Versus Femininity
This dimension describes societies where people are more "masculine" in their approach to life—more task- and achievement-oriented—or more "feminine"—more relationship- and care-oriented.

On one side of the axis, we see cultures that are masculine-oriented, such as the USA, Norway, the UK, and Germany, where material success, ambition, achievement, competition, progress, and winning are dominant values. Failure is a disaster. Bigger and faster are better. Men are supposed to be ambitious, assertive, and tough. Women should be subservient and tender. Conflict is resolved by arguing or fighting.

On the other side of the axis are feminine cultures, such as Indonesia, Spain, and Thailand. They take care of the weak and sick. Small is beautiful. Everybody is supposed to be modest, softly spoken, and empathetic. Achievements are played down; quality of life is more important. Conflicts are resolved through compromise.

Weak Versus Strong Uncertainty Avoidance

This dimension is about how change and uncertainty are approached in different societies—how anxious members of a society are about the unknown, and how they attempt to cope with this anxiety by minimizing uncertainty.

On one side of the axis we see cultures such as Germany, Switzerland, and Austria that require stability and have created structures, such as laws and policies, that help to maintain routine and normality. In cultures with strong uncertainty avoidance people prefer explicit rules and formally structured activities. A common belief is that without rules, things will not work. There are rigid taboos around certain subjects, and ambiguity, change, and the unknown are treated with suspicion.

On the other side of the axis are cultures such as Brazil, Israel, and India, societies that are capable of tolerating change and uncertainty and accepting difference. In these cultures, people prefer implicit, flexible rules or guidelines, and informal activities. Rules are limited, and can be broken if something better comes along.

This orientation is likely to affect how foreigners are treated. Cultures with strong uncertainty avoidance are likely to treat foreigners with suspicion, and thus, as a newcomer, you may have to endure stares, remarks, prejudice, and discrimination.

Long- Versus Short-Term Orientation

This dimension describes the ways in which time is perceived and how this perception is played out in everyday life.

On one side of the axis, we see cultures that are future-oriented societies. People in these cultures tend to work hard for future results, talk about delayed gratification, and are very persistent when they pursue a goal. Traditions and the past are also important. This often translates into linearity: schedules, timetables, and long-term plans are important. People are task-oriented, stick to procedures, and behave appropriately. Examples of such cultures are Germany, the USA, and the UK.

On the other side of the axis are present-focused cultures, in which people think more about now than about the future. Life is about living in the now, getting quick results, and enjoying the moment. In these societies, people value actions and attitudes that produce immediate results: immediate stability, saving face, and reciprocation of greetings, favors, and gifts. This often goes hand-in-hand with a multilinear approach: unpredictable timetables, one project influences another, frequent changes of plan, juggling facts, pulling strings to get things done more quickly, and multitasking. Examples of such cultures are Spain, Brazil, Italy, and Israel.

The following exercise, which is based on Hofstede's cultural dimensions, can help you to identify the differences between your homeland culture and that of your destination country.

✍ ASSESSING CULTURAL DIFFERENCES EXERCISE

Below are five continuums. Simply assess where on each axis your homeland culture is positioned, and where your host culture is. Mark the positions. This will enable you to see more clearly where the cultural gaps are likely to be.

1. Power distance

Small power distance   Large power distance

◀————————————————————————▶

2. Individualism versus collectivism

Individualism   Collectivism

◀————————————————————————▶

3. Masculinity versus femininity

Masculinity   Femininity

◀————————————————————————▶

4. Weak versus strong uncertainty avoidance

Weak uncertainty avoidance   Strong uncertainty avoidance

◀————————————————————————▶

5. Long- versus short-term orientation

Short-term orientation   Long-term orientation

◀————————————————————————▶

6. What have you learned from this exercise?

_____

_____

_____

_____

_____

Essential Culture-Specific Knowledge

In your initial introduction to the host country's culture, I recommend that you focus on and familiarize yourself with the following cultural rules:

❑ Dress codes: what is the appropriate dress for men, women, and children in different situations? What is not acceptable, or considered offensive?

❑ Greetings and salutations: what are the usual forms of address between strangers? Acquaintances? Friends? Men and women? How formal should you be in different situations? When and with whom are handshakes, hugs, and kisses used?

❑ Personal space: what is considered a comfortable space between people? What is appropriate in terms of touching, eye contact, and body positioning?

❑ Daily schedule: what are the usual timings of daily routines, such as working or business hours, family times, times for shopping, banking, schooling, sleeping? When are shops, offices, banks, and other places closed, for example on weekends, public holidays, and religious festivals?

❑ Family and partnership conduct: what are the norms among family members when at home and when in public? How are your marital or sexual choices likely to be treated?

❑ Neighborly conduct: what duties do people have toward their neighbors? What rules apply with regard to children, noise levels, trash, pets, parking? What level of acquaintance can you expect? Are there any introduction protocols?

❑ Alcohol and smoking: what is considered legal or illegal, and what are the social rules regarding alcohol, smoking, and drug usage?

Learning how to manage differences and adapt cross-culturally will pay off in a great many ways. You will not only gain insight into another way of life, but you will also become more relaxed and comfortable personally, and more effective and successful in your work. You will have acquired a set of skills that will enable you to adapt more easily to any new cultural environment. Along the way, you will also gain valuable insights into yourself and your own culture.

Chapter 8

THE CROSS-CULTURAL ADAPTATION PROCESS

Our lives are filled with countless transitions: when we mature and age; when we enter a new school or go to college; when we change jobs; when we marry or have children; when we move to a new home or relocate to a different country. All of these life changes and numerous others require us to adjust to new conditions.

The process of adjusting to new settings, circumstances, positions, or roles can be demanding, stressful, and, at times, painful. However, once we have become acclimatized to our new situation we realize that we have grown tremendously, not only in our perspective, but also in our capacity to handle change, diversity, and uncertainty.

The adjustment required of those who relocate internationally is extensive and immediate. Faced all at once with the task of building the details of life in the new place, as well as adjusting to a different climate, geography, food, currency, language, and culture, those who relocate must adapt and perform quickly.

Moving to and living in a new country brings many changes in our lives, and at the same time it exposes us to a different culture. And it is this double-edged challenge that triggers culture shock. But it is also what makes the cross-cultural adaptation process a journey of personal transformation.

> The cross-cultural adaptation process is a learning process, through which travelers acquire the knowledge to enable them to function in their new environment.

In the course of the cross-cultural adaptation process, travelers acquire three types of knowledge:

+ The practical aspects of the new environment: how to get to places, where to find things, how to do things.
+ The cultural aspects of the new environment: local norms and customs, how things are done, how people behave, what is considered "proper" behavior. It also includes shared beliefs and values—what is considered important and what is valued.
+ Language and communication: the language used in the new country, jargon and slang, and how people communicate—tone, volume, body language, formality, informality; and the preferred means of communication, such as face-to-face, e-mail, and telephone.

The diagram below displays a typical cross-cultural learning curve drawn over a period of ten years.

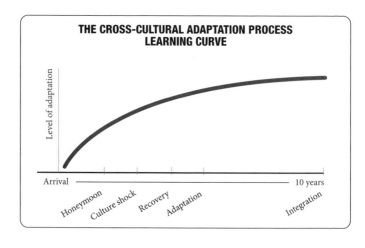

Note how steep the learning curve is at the beginning—in the first months of relocation. Then it flattens, when people adapt and integrate. Therefore, the main learning processes occur during the first months of relocation, in the honeymoon, culture-shock, and recovery phases.

In fact, significant learning takes place during the culture-shock period, and there is a strong correlation between the culture-shock experience and the learning that takes place at that point. It is the rapid learning itself that triggers the culture-shock experience.

Most people cannot help but react to all the new learning and stimuli now present in their lives. Their reaction takes the form not of one particular emotional occurrence, but of a series of episodes made up of a mixture of emotions, ranging from euphoria to depression and from fascination to homesickness. This mixed bag of reactions is very common, and a normal part of the process of adaptation.

In spite of its complexity, from a psychological point of view, the adaptation process is remarkably predictable. The process often begins on a high note—the honeymoon phase—then sinks into culture shock, and finally, recovery, adjustment, and integration. This is known as "the U-shaped cultural adaptation process," and is illustrated below.

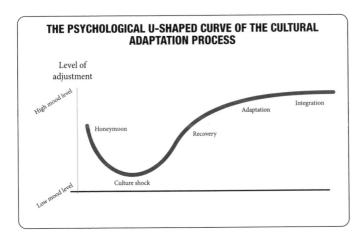

THE PSYCHOLOGICAL U-SHAPED CURVE OF THE CULTURAL ADAPTATION PROCESS

Not everyone experiences these stages in exactly the same way, but most travelers will go through the highs and lows, the positive and the negative aspects of living in a new culture. Some people may skip stages or move through them quickly.

How you may experience these phases will depend greatly on the type and scope of your preparation. Nevertheless, change is more difficult for some than for others. It is therefore important to be patient, and with time you will reach the final stage of adjustment.

The cross-cultural adaptation process described here is a much studied and well-understood phenomenon. Books have been written about it, and there are workshops and seminars that advise people how to cope with it.

Here is where the difficulty is: most of us are ill equipped for this journey and the demands it will make on us. The ability to function in another culture takes more than knowledge. It requires the development of a cross-cultural outlook, which enables you to look behind behavior and events to uncover what they mean. It requires behavioral flexibility—the ability to adjust your own behavior to accommodate your surroundings, and an ability to manage your own psychological state to address some of the challenges involved in cultural adjustment. Without these abilities we can live in another culture as outsiders for years, unable to access a world that seems unapproachable and incomprehensible.

> Though it may be distressing and disrupting, the cross-cultural experience, is, for most people, a very valuable one—a mind-stretching process that will leave you with a broader perspective, profound insights into yourself, and open-mindedness about other cultures and people.

It is an opportunity to challenge yourself to go beyond your comfort zone: to stretch your thinking and behavior, widen your perspective, become more flexible and tolerant toward yourself and others, and sharpen your reflective and analytic skills.

Chapter 9

MANAGING THE TRANSITION

The four to eight weeks just before your flight are considered the transitional period. This phase includes the packing and shipping, the farewell parties, handling flight arrangements, and making last-minute preparations. It ends when you board your plane.

Although it is a brief phase that lasts only a few weeks, it can be very demanding, both physically and mentally. There is obviously a lot going on, and often there is little time for rest, never mind reflection. You may feel you are constantly driving at top speed, with your foot on the accelerator, and that in itself is very tiring. You are also aware that a similar process awaits you in your destination country!

As soon as the shippers have taken your belongings, your home no longer feels like home, and, as you say good-bye to all the familiar people and places in your life, you may feel the losses and realize the full impact of your move.

The relocation day brings this phase to a close. However, it may add its own emotional tone. For most people the relocation day brings both sadness about the life they leave behind and excitement about the future.

Much of the difficulty that this period presents arises from being in an in-between phase, where you are pulled out of your comfort zone, and at this point in your journey you have not yet connected to your new environment. You may acutely recognize that now you have no comfort zone: you are constantly living in your "stretch" or even "panic" zone.

The main action to take, as a way of easing the psychological strains of this phase, is to look after yourself, and to do what you can to make this period as comfortable as possible for yourself and your family.

In what follows I will highlight the main events and some of the hurdles you may face in this period. There are also some powerful dos and don'ts, which can help you and your family keep the stress and turmoil that emerge to the minimum, and smooth your path to successful adaptation.

Many preparation and change management strategies are offered here, to give you a head start and help you manage your transition and adaptation more effectively. As you go through your journey, however, you will find that the most valuable tool here is knowledge. This knowledge allows you to anticipate what lies ahead, to prepare yourself for certain events and situations, and to have the confidence to take appropriate action when they happen.

SOMETHING TO REMEMBER
"Every change, even a change for the better, is always accompanied by drawbacks and discomforts."
Arnold Bennett

Chapter 10

PACKING UP YOUR HOME

> Whether you are relocating reluctantly
> or happily and hopefully, your move will entail losses
> on the way to making gains, and one of the most obvious
> losses incurred during the transition phase
> is the loss of your home.

Your home is much more than just where you live. It's your safe haven, where you feel protected and comfortable, and where you can be yourself and express yourself. Home is the place where you belong. It may be saturated with your memories.

During the transition period, and when you are preparing for the shipment of your belongings, your home begins to take a different form—and then it is emptied. This is the point where many people begin to feel the extent of their losses. Some, though, don't realize how much their home means to them until after they move.

If you are deeply attached to your home, and if your feeling of continuity is grounded in the physical structure, leaving it can push you into a state of psychological homelessness. You may grieve, or feel sad, lost, and anxious, for weeks, even months. Even if you are not deeply attached to your home, it is a place where you probably feel competent. You know where things are and how things work, and can find your way around in the dark. Moving ruptures this sense of mastery. You may feel helpless, confused, and incompetent. This, in turn, can cause your confidence to slump.

Many people have a strong need for order, predictability, and control. They are likely to feel anxious and depressed when their physical environment, belongings, and daily routines change. It is important, therefore, to acknowledge that the preparation for shipping, the packing, and clearing, and the shipping day itself, entail not only the physical work that needs to be done, but also a strong emotional reaction.

During the Transition Period
✦ Be conscious of the emotional issues emerging during packing and shipping.
✦ Allow yourself the time to acknowledge and validate your emotions.
✦ Remember that feeling sad or stressed doesn't mean that you are having doubts about your relocation. It just means you are normal!

The following tips will help you manage the packing and shipment, and relieve the emotional turmoil that you may experience during this phase.

TIMING YOUR SHIPMENT
A question I am often asked in relation to the shipment is, "When is the best time to ship?" Your shipment might take weeks, or even months, to arrive in your destination country. Therefore, you have a choice between:
✦ Having the shippers collect your belongings early, perhaps a few weeks before your flight, and either staying in your home (if possible) or finding temporary accommodation locally.
✦ Scheduling your shipment as close as possible to your relocation day, which means that you may need to live rough for a while, or rent furnished temporary accommodation, in your destination country.

Tempting as it may be to maintain your normal household routines for as long as possible, it is probably a better plan to ship early, so that your household items will arrive soon after your move. Living without belongings is much easier in your homeland, where everything else is familiar and comfortable, and where you have support, than in a foreign place.

Sending the shipment early also has the advantage of providing a breathing space between the hectic sorting and packing and your flight, in which you can unwind and focus on visiting friends and saying good-bye.

Often a house becomes unlivable once it is emptied, and in this case, I would recommend renting temporary accommodation in your homeland.

Some people find it difficult to stay in their house once the shipment has been taken, not because it is unlivable, but because of the emotional upheaval involved in acknowledging the loss of their home. If this is true for you, I recommend that you stay with family or friends or rent temporary accommodation between your shipment day and your flight.

MAKING A PACKING PLAN

As you prepare for your move and say good-bye to friends and family, you will also have to pack your belongings and attempt to fit the entire contents of your home into a removal van, and then into cargo crates. This can be an exhausting process. Even though you may be donating, selling, or throwing out clothing, furniture, and other items, you will be surprised to see how many belongings you have accumulated over the years.

The best time to begin planning for your packing and shipping is three to six months before your move. This will give you enough time to contact movers and research the options they can offer you, dispose of unwanted items, decide what to ship and what to take with you on the flight, organize items for the shippers to pack, and pack some items yourself.

A packing plan can help to reduce stress and allow you to have more control over the situation. Outlining a plan early is the best way to avoid having to rush or having sleepless nights toward the end of the period in an attempt to get it all done before the shipper steps in.

Starting early and working slowly through the packing also gives you the time you may need to deal with the emotional aspects of the shipment.

While your plan doesn't have to be extensive, it should include some of the following:

❑ A list of shipping companies to call for quotes. Ask about their services, policies, insurance provisions, and schedule before you hire them. Ensure they can offer you a door-to-door service, including storage and customs clearing.

❑ A list of those items that you are allowed to bring into your destination country and those that are prohibited, according to customs regulations.

❑ A note of weight and size restrictions for household shipments, air freight, and personal luggage.

❑ A list of electrical items that are compatible with your destination country.

❑ A list of the items you plan to take with you on your flight.

❑ A shopping list of items that are not available in your destination country that you wish to buy and ship.

❑ A list of documents to photocopy.

❑ Most international shipping companies will not allow you to pack items yourself because of insurance regulations, but if they do, list the items you intend to pack yourself.

❑ A reasonable timeframe for sorting your belongings and preparing those to be shipped. Ensure that you leave enough time to organize everything without feeling rushed off your feet.

❑ Consider the following categories for sorting:
  • Flight luggage
  • Items to ship (make inventories for insurance purposes)
  • Items to leave in a safe place or with trusted relatives
  • Items to store locally
  • Items to give to family or friends
  • Items to donate to charities
  • Items to sell
  • Items to throw away
  • Items you need to use until the shipment day, and consumables. Of these, list those that will eventually be

shipped, and any consumables that you intend to take with you on your flight.

❑ A plan of which rooms and cupboards you intend to begin sorting first, second, and last.

❑ A labeling system that will enable you to mark clearly the rooms and areas that you have already sorted.

❑ A space to store boxes and bags.

❑ An empty space or room where you can store items that should not be shipped.

❑ Your shipper will instruct you where to place items that are to be shipped. In my experience it is easiest to put things back in their cupboards so that the shipper can pack them from there.

❑ If you are packing any items yourself, you will need a space to put these once they are packed and ready to ship.

❑ A timetable for all the people involved in the packing. When will they be coming? For how long? The costs involved, if any, and what they are required to do.

Some tips on packing

❑ Before inviting shippers to give you a quote, attempt to separate the things that you do not wish to ship, and move them aside from everything else. This will enable the shipper to assess the volume of the shipment and give you a more accurate quote.

❑ Ask the shipper for clear instructions on how to prepare items for shipping and where you should put them ready for packing.

❑ If you are packing yourself, ensure you comply with insurance regulations.

❑ If packing items yourself, beware of over-packing. This can cause boxes to break and can cause back injury.

❑ Lifting boxes should be done carefully. Always lift from the knees, and don't attempt to lift something that is too heavy.

❑ Once you have placed your belongings in boxes ensure you label the boxes clearly.

❑ When moving items from attics or closets, wear a face mask to prevent inhaling dust, debris, and mold.

❑ Allow children to decide what they want to take with them, and what to ship. This gives them some sense of control over the situation, which enables them to assume responsibility and be part of the relocation journey.

❑ When you ship clothes, towels, bedding, and curtains, make sure they are clean. Otherwise, they will smell!

❑ Remove batteries from items you are intending to ship, to prevent leakage of battery fluid and consequent damage.

❑ Large items, such as furniture, are likely to be taken apart. Unless you have arranged otherwise with the shipping company, you will have to assemble these again yourself. Consider this point when employing the shipping company, and when deciding what to ship.

❑ If you are considering selling items at a garage sale, or online, do this well in advance of your shipping day, so that these things are cleared out in good time.

❑ Before packing electrical goods, find out whether they will be compatible in your new country. Items such as DVD players, televisions, and phones may not work there. For smaller items obtain electrical adapters and attach them to the appliances before shipping.

Bite-Size Packing

This is how a family with four children, who recently relocated from the UK, dealt with the task of sorting and clearing their house, and how they prepared for the shipment.

They began several months before their shipment day. They targeted a room to sort and clear, and scheduled two hours each day for all the family to work together to clear the room. When they were working in each room, they sorted out items in the following way:

✦ Items to throw out, which they bagged and put out with the garbage or recycling.

✦ Items to give to family, friends, or charities, which they packed up, labeled, and put aside.

✦ Items to sell, which they moved into a different room in preparation for the sale.

✦ Items ready to ship, which they stacked on designated shelves ready for the shippers to pack. They marked the shelves with red "*Ship*" stickers.
✦ Items to take on the flight. They stacked these on separate shelves marked with blue "*Flight*" stickers.
✦ Items required for use before the move. These were consumables, linen, kitchen utensils, and other things that they intended to ship or take on the flight but that they needed in the meantime. They put them on shelves marked with a "smiley" sticker. On the day of the shipment, some of these were packed to ship, and others were packed to go into flight luggage.

This system allowed the family to get things done on time, with no stress or backaches, and helped them to keep everything tidy and organized. This is a great example of how you can break down what initially seems like an overwhelming task into smaller chunks. This made the task manageable, practical, and efficient.

An issue that all travelers face is the question of what to take with them on the flight and what to ship. One of the most common mistakes that I have witnessed is to say, "Let's ship whatever we can, and what doesn't go in the shipment we'll take with us!" Well, Lena's story, below, shows that this may not be the best way to go about it!

Two Children and Ten Suitcases
Lena's Story
One of my worst relocation mistakes was to plan to stay with two young children and ten suitcases for a period of two weeks in what was considered a relatively large family room in a London hotel.

The problem was that the room was not as big as I had expected. In fact, it was small, even for a family with almost no luggage.

It was a very unpleasant experience. It felt crowded, tight, and stuffy, and as soon as we opened a suitcase there was very little room to move around. Every space was filled with toys, food and drink, clothes, and other items. The only place where the kids could play was on the beds. It felt like a prison cell.

Every attempt to go out took considerable time just to find the items we needed, simply because opening one suitcase meant we had to close the others.

Within twenty-four hours we were all snappy, cross, and emotionally drained. We were constantly clashing and shouting at each other. The children were moody, clingy, and whining. All I wanted to do was get on the first plane home!

Not a great start to a new life, was it?

What to Ship and What to Take on Your Flight

+ Pack the things you will need for your initial stay abroad, ensure they fit in your flight luggage, and ship the rest.
+ Think of your first accommodation when packing. What will you need to make it comfortable? How big is the living space?
+ Pack according to your needs and the available space in your first lodging. If your space will be relatively small (such as a hotel room, or a room with relatives), take as little as possible with you.

The only circumstances in which it would make sense to take more luggage with you on the flight are if your first accommodation is relatively large, if there is storage space that you can use, or if you are going straight to your own home, whether rented or owned.

Comfort Items

During the first days or weeks in the new country you are likely to feel tired, stressed, and disoriented. There are three categories of items that you can take with you in your luggage that can help to alleviate your stress and support your settling-in period:

+ Items that solve practical problems, such as a first-aid kit, bottled water, cell phones, cash.
+ Comfort items that help you and your family relieve the stress, soothe your nerves, and create a sense of

security. It could be your children's beloved blankets or toys, a book, a particular type of tea or coffee, or chocolate. Any habit or comfort item that works for you is worthwhile.

✦ Items that help you create a sense of home during the early weeks of the transition. These are familiar objects, such as family photos, mugs, tablecloths, or anything else that will help you feel more at home in your new environment.

THE SHIPMENT DAY
Some tips for managing the shipment day

❏ Before the shippers arrive, make sure that you have separated and marked the items that go into the shipment and into your flight luggage. Put the flight luggage where the shippers have no access. Remove things that you intend to leave in the house that should not be shipped.

❏ When they arrive, show the shippers through the house, specifying what items are to be packed, and pointing out any items that need particular care.

❏ Where possible, arrange for your children to stay out of the house for the day.

❏ Lay in some snacks and drinks for the day. If you have packed your dishes and utensils to ship, get some disposable cutlery and plates.

❏ Have sufficient rest the day before to minimize the stress.

❏ Packers work very fast! It is best to keep out of their way.

❏ During the packing, the house will get dusty and dirty. If you are staying in the house, keep some cleaning items out, or borrow some from a neighbor.

❏ Once all items have been packed, take a final walk around to ensure that everything has been included. Remember to check behind doors and inside cupboards.

❏ Some companies may require you to sign an inventory of all the items they have loaded. Check through this to ensure you are satisfied.

Shippers' Blunders

In one of my own international shipments, the shipper simply packed a vase of fresh flowers (and water)! Perhaps he thought they were artificial. Luckily for me, he packed it so well that nothing else was damaged.

A friend of mine had a box full of trash packed and shipped. Can you imagine what it looked like—and smelled like—a month later, when she unpacked it?

HOW TO EASE THE TRANSITION PHASE

✦ Follow your relocation plan. Leave as little as possible to do at this stage. Try to finish all other things beforehand.

✦ Wherever you can, delegate! Get other people to do the work.

✦ Make a conscious effort to make this period as comfortable as possible for you and your family. Have proper meals, find time to be with your loved ones, unwind, and rest.

✦ Take care of details. Small habits are important at this point. Find the comfort items or habits that make you feel good, and stick to them amid the change (see detailed explanation of this strategy in Chapter 13).

✦ When your normal schedule is interrupted, create temporary routines that make you feel comfortable and in control, and stick to them throughout the period (see Chapter 13).

Chapter 11

THE FAREWELL STAGE

Every entrance has involved an exit, and the farewell stage is very much about recognizing and coming to terms with the costs of your exit. International relocation is, without a doubt, a move permeated with significant losses.

The farewell stage has three aspects:

+ Saying good-bye to special people in your life: family and friends, neighbors, colleagues, employees, teachers, nannies, and others.
+ Parting from familiar places: your home, your office, the children's school, a local park, the gym, your favorite coffee shop, the beach.
+ Leaving special items behind: such as your car, your piano, or other items that you can't take with you.

Good-byes are sometimes welcome! Leaving an abusive partner, a nagging mother-in-law, a critical boss, or a stressful job, street crime, or harsh weather conditions can be a cause for celebration, and those may well be some of the reasons for your wish to move. But it is rare to find movers whose good-byes are not accompanied by some sadness.

Whether felt before the move, immediately afterward, or months later, grief and pain are the normal responses to the myriad losses that your move entails. You may feel angry, fearful, lonely, and sad. You may be disappointed in yourself. You may find yourself flooded with grief, and longing for what you have lost.

Saying good-bye and acknowledging your feelings about leaving will help you to close this chapter of your life and move on to the next. It is therefore important to allow yourself to grieve.

Remember: grieving or feeling sad or stressed does not
mean that your decision to relocate is a mistake.
It just means you are human!

As soon as you realize that your future won't include all these
special people, places, and things, a process of grieving is set in
motion, and it can be intense. It may take you by surprise,
especially if you are happy about the move. You may mistakenly
think that something is wrong with you. The pain may bring
doubts about the move. If you are unprepared for the grief and
interpret it as a sign of inadequacy, it may tip you into depression.

GOOD GRIEF
Grief is a psychological state, not an emotion.
It includes sadness, longing, and sometimes anger at
the person or circumstances responsible for your loss.
Grief is different from depression. It is a state of sadness
provoked by loss. Depression is a state of diminished
self-worth, provoked by failure.

The first stage of grieving is is anticipatory grief—sadness at
the prospect of loss, and longing to hold on to what you are
about to lose. Later there may be sadness and longing to
recapture what was lost. Old sorrows may also reappear.

Grief is painful, and some people naturally seek ways to
avoid it. Some people deliberately turn their thoughts away
from impending losses. Others may try to reason grief away.
For some, the surge of activity—sorting, packing, and
dismantling their home, organizing things, and focusing on
preparation—can stimulate an emotional high that masks the
grief about impending losses.

Grieving is a necessary process for emotional health. Those
who cage their grief become vulnerable and may experience
explosive eruptions later. Unacknowledged grief can express
itself in indirect ways through fatigue, depression, and illness.

GRIEVING IS CONSTRUCTIVE
Grieving allows you to let go of people, places, and things,
and helps you to move on. Allow yourself to feel the
sadness. Go through the rituals of farewell: visit special
places and hold good-bye parties. Tears may flow,
but these are healing tears.

For many of us, the loss or our home and special people,
places, and things in our lives stirs and ruptures something
deep inside us—our sense of self, and our sense of place.

Our identities are expressed and confirmed through all
these aspects: our belongings, our home, and other special
places in our life; our profession or job; the roles we play, that
express our capabilities and give meaning to our life; the
familiar structure of our life; the rhythm of our routines that
create a sense of place and security. Relocation shatters all these
aspects, and after the move time and energy will be needed to
regain the familiar details and rhythms of daily life that are so
vital to our sense of self.

Dealing With Sadness
When the sadness wells up:

✦ Consider what helps you to feel cozy and safe. A cup of
coffee or tea? A hot bath? Some favorite music? A book?
Once you identify your sources of comfort, claim them.

✦ Let others know what you need to ease this stressful
time.

✦ Grief often includes anxiety and anger. Physical release,
such as going for a jog, riding a bike, or walking, can
alleviate these feelings.

✦ Talk about your troubled feelings with others. You
need to feel understood and supported.

✦ You may find it helpful to keep a journal.

✦ Keep the lines of communication open with your
nearest and dearest, so that the sadness can bring you
together rather than draw you apart.

GOOD-BYE TO SPECIAL PEOPLE

The focus of the farewell phase is on relationships. What becomes apparent when you go through this phase are the costs and changes that are likely to take place in these ties once you relocate. Both you and those you leave behind may fear that your relocation will bring the relationship to its end.

Don't deny the changes that are likely to occur in the nature of your ties. Changes will take place, but that doesn't mean the relationships are lost. In fact, most people keep some of their ties in their homeland for years to come, and sometimes for life.

One of the difficulties of the farewell stage is that the places and things you are leaving behind won't criticize or blame you for inflicting pain on others, but some *people* around you will!

Your family and friends may be ambivalent about your move. They may be happy for you, and want to support you, but at the same time may feel abandoned, sad, and resentful. They may well be interpreting your departure as, "You don't care about me anymore." They, too, will need time to grieve and heal, just as you do.

It is important that you find ways to show your loved ones that you do care, and to reassure them that your relationship with them is strong and resilient, and that it can and will be maintained, despite the distance. Empathize and be patient with people who are reacting negatively.

Essential Steps to Maintain Your Ties
+ Update your address, e-mail, and phone lists.
+ Prepare a list of people to whom you will need to send a "change of address" note in due course.
+ Make a calendar of birthdays and other important dates.
+ Get a cell phone that works internationally during your first period abroad, and give the number to your relatives and friends.

✦ Plan ways to keep in touch with those left behind
  through e-mail, phone, Skype, and social media
  networks.
✦ Schedule set times for phone calls.
✦ Make plans for mutual visits, and share these plans
  with those around you.

FAREWELL PARTIES

Farewell parties are important transition ceremonies that are
designed to help you come to terms with your departure and
create closure.

Some people prefer a big party; some prefer a small party,
or a few small ones. Some have the party at home; some have
other people host it for them; some rent a hall.

In some communities it is customary to exchange gifts
before the departure, or at the farewell party. In others, people
will give you a going-away gift.

Do what is right for you, and what you feel comfortable with.

How to Ease the Good-bye Stage

✦ Acknowledge the changes that are likely to occur in
  your relationships. Don't dismiss them.
✦ Reassure your family and friends that your relationship
  can and will be maintained.
✦ Empathize with people who are reacting negatively.
✦ Take responsibility for the changes that you are about
  to introduce into your relationships, and work to
  rebuild them.
✦ Focus on creating ways and means to support your
  relationships and ensure their continuity.

LEAVING SPECIAL PLACES AND BELONGINGS

This part of the farewell stage involves leaving our familiar
surroundings—our house, the neighborhood, the local shops,
the mall, the school—and the items that we can't take with us.
For some people, it is also about leaving images of their past,

childhood memories, the neighborhood where they grew up, their parents' home, their school, and the graves of loved ones.

Some people find this as difficult as saying good-bye to people. Many don't expect to feel sad and nostalgic, and are taken by surprise.

The focus of this phase is, therefore, on how you relate to these things that currently have a physical presence in your life, and on how you convert them in your mind into a symbol—an image of what they are, and what they mean to you.

How to Ease the Leaving

✦ Self-awareness and sharing helps!
✦ A common response is to become immersed in action and doing. This leads to a delayed farewell.
✦ Visit the places you want to say good-bye to.
✦ Take photos, and create a diary or scrapbook of the places and items you want to remember.
✦ Write down or shoot videos of the memories that are related to the items or places.
✦ Collect typical items from places you want to remember.

Chapter 12

THE RELOCATION DAY

The relocation day is, for most people, an emotional roller-coaster ride, provoking a mixture of sadness and excitement.

In the interviews I have conducted with travelers, many said that before the flight, when making their last arrangements, they felt fine. They were tired, even exhausted, physically, but nevertheless ready to go. Some felt stressed or sad.

For those who were saying a last farewell—parting from the people closest to them—at home or at the airport, this was an emotional and tearful moment.

On the flight, some became energized again. Others were emotional and reflective, and some slept through the entire flight. By the time they landed, most felt slightly stressed, but generally enthusiastic and hopeful.

The next part—dealing with the bureaucratic aspect of their relocation—was not so pleasant. Since few people enjoy red tape and long lines, most felt that their level of energy dropped to "OK" (or even below that), as they went through immigration and customs.

One of the things that made a huge difference to the way this day was experienced was when someone would be waiting for them at the airport—relatives, friends, a mentor, relocation consultant, or even a taxi driver. I found that the people who had someone meeting them started their journey with a more positive outlook than those who didn't. If you do have people meeting you, though, ensure you arrange some way of communicating with them as they wait, and alert them when they need to come and pick you up.

By the evening, most travelers were tired, yet eager, and positive about it all.

SAYING GOOD-BYE AT THE AIRPORT

For most travelers, the good-byes at the airport are about parting from the people who are your closest friends and family members. This is generally the low point of the day.

Some of my trainees knew that this was going to be an emotional event that was likely to be difficult for everybody—especially for elderly relatives and children—but despite this they wanted to go through the experience and to be fully present emotionally because they felt that this was their way to honor these relationships.

Others feared that driving together and parting at the airport in tears would be too much to take, either for them, or for those left behind. They found various ways around this:

✦ Some people, particularly those traveling with young children, asked close relatives to come with them on the flight and stay with them during the first weeks of arrival. One couple bought tickets for their parents as a going-away gift, and found their presence invaluable. It enabled them to focus on the settling-in arrangements while the grandparents took care of their children.

✦ Parents, siblings, or friends who escorted travelers on their relocation day and stayed with them during the first weeks also found the experience helpful. They were able to experience and witness the move and were often relieved to watch their loved ones settle in. Also, the fact that the mover required their help took them out of the "person who is left behind" position, and placed them in the role of helper, which made a huge difference to how they related to the person who was moving.

✦ Some travelers arranged for family or friends to arrive a few weeks later to visit. This eliminated the sadness of the farewell on the relocation day, and delayed it to when the relatives went back home.

✦ Another way of addressing this was to invite parents, relatives, or friends to stay the night before, and spend time with them that evening, but ask them not to come to the airport.

✦ I met several families who made a stopover trip on the way to their new destination. Some had their extended families join them at a resort, and from there each flew in a different direction.

Think about these strategies, and find the way that is going to be the least upsetting both for you and for others.

A STOPOVER TRIP

A stopover trip can be a welcome break from the hassles of the transition period. It can provide a valuable breathing space after the stress of the shipment and before the settling-in period, and can help you arrive in your new country with a fresh, rested, and energetic attitude, ready to take on the challenges ahead.

On the other hand, if you are not in the mood for a vacation and are eager to settle in, or if you are moving with young children and have spent some time in temporary housing, a stopover trip may be an unwelcome distraction.

Do what is best for you and your family.

Chapter 13

SOFT LANDING

**GET EXCITED! IT'S THE FIRST DAY
OF YOUR NEW LIFE**
Travelers seldom appreciate the meaning attached to the
first day of their relocation. In my interviews with clients,
I found that those who treated their first day abroad as a
special day, and took the time to celebrate it, had a much
more pleasant relocation experience throughout than those
who spent their first day sleeping, standing in lines at the
bank or the supermarket, or dealing with red tape.

> To begin your relocation journey
> on the right foot, take time to celebrate:
> have some fun, do something pleasurable or exciting,
> and make your first day memorable!

Many people still remember their relocation day in detail
years later, and some celebrate the anniversary every year.

The following exercise is designed to help you think about
and plan the first day of your relocation.

PLANNING YOUR FIRST DAY ABROAD EXERCISE

1. What would you like to do on the first day of your relocation?

2. What will make your first day abroad special and memorable?

3. What would you like to avoid? What could spoil the day?

YOUR FIRST WEEK ABROAD: REST AND RECHARGE

The majority of travelers experience physical and mental fatigue on arrival. Even if you didn't stay up late packing or cleaning, finishing projects, or attending farewell parties, you may be exhausted and jet-lagged from the trip.

Your main concern during your first week of arrival should be your and your family's health, safety, and comfort. All other settling-in arrangements, pressing as they may seem, can wait!

> Your priority upon arrival is to rest,
> recuperate, and stay healthy.

A continuous state of fatigue will make you more prone to illness, less effective, and more irritable. Illness and exhaustion can deplete morale, souring your attitude toward your move.

If you have been sent abroad to work by your company, arriving just before a weekend or taking a few days off is recommended.

If your move takes you to a different time zone, make a conscious effort to adjust to your new time frame as quickly as possible. To overcome jet-lag quickly, the "forced wake-up" method is very useful. This involves waking up at a reasonable time in the morning, staying active during the day (and where possible exposing yourself to sunlight), and keeping yourself awake until a reasonable bedtime. A few days of "forced wake-up" should adjust your biological clock.

In addition to fatigue, your body may be exposed to new environmental conditions such as harsh weather, biting insects, unfamiliar food, and new germs. Colds, upset stomachs, and skin problems are common after arrival in a new country.

> To avoid or minimize illness, adjust gradually
> to unfamiliar food and water.

Some tips for managing your initial adjustment:

✦ Be sure that you have appropriate clothing for the local weather.

✦ Check that your first accommodation provides the necessary safety measures, weather control systems, and small comforts you need to allow you to recuperate and replenish your strength.

✦ Try to avoid visiting areas where you may be exposed to unfamiliar plants and insects.

✦ During your first weeks, go carefully with food and drink. Seek out familiar foods, and drink bottled water.

✦ In areas where water and food may be contaminated, avoid salads and other raw foods. Make sure you follow food disinfection guidelines. Wash your hands often as a measure to prevent disease.

Safety First!

✦ Be more vigilant than usual. Take responsibility for your family's safety.

✦ Learn how to keep safe on the streets and indoors.

✦ Find out what to do in emergency situations.

✦ Carefully observe and follow hygiene guidelines to avoid contaminated food and water.

✦ Identify local hospitals and arrange meetings with doctors and dentists as soon as you arrive. Don't wait for an emergency!

✦ If you can't read labels or instructions on consumable or household items such as foods, cleaning solutions, and medicines, don't use them!

Chapter 14

THE HONEYMOON

> Often, when a person relocates to a foreign country,
> he or she experiences a "honeymoon" phase
> of exploration and discovery.

This period is characterized by great expectations, excitement, and euphoria. All seems new and alluring, and you may feel eager and inquisitive about everything that you can observe, discover, do, and experience.

You may have been dreaming about this time for months, or even years, and now that you are finally here, you may feel a sense of victory and achievement.

Many of my clients say that, despite the physical fatigue, psychologically they felt recharged and energized, highly motivated, and ready and eager for what they envisioned as an exciting adventure—my new life!

This period can feel like an extended vacation. If you have acquaintances or business connections, you may be invited out or to come over, asked to join other leisure or social activities, or taken sightseeing. You may come across many interesting new places and customs, and the "tourist feeling" may stay with you for some time.

While some travelers experience a sense of relief to be away from the day-to-day stresses of their life back home, others may experience a deeper sense of freedom, feeling that this is a chance to make a new life, and that everything is possible. This sense may also emanate from the fact that they are now free from all sorts of social or cultural restrictions— of their homeland, and of their host country. There is no one from home to monitor their behavior, and, since the local people consider them visitors, they are not expected to understand local laws—and thus their errors are likely to be treated by the locals with humor, or ignored and forgiven.

During this early phase of the adaptation process, the similarities between the home culture and the host culture are more noticeable than the differences. Almost everywhere around the globe people share some routines and practices—they get married, raise children, work, shop, play, cook, eat, and relax. This gives the newcomer a sense of reassurance. Although you may well notice some differences, at this point these are likely to be perceived as interesting, but not too much of a problem.

Additionally, many people seem to notice the advantages of life in the new place and the benefits of their move. The tendency to focus on the benefits and advantages can be explained by a psychological phenomenon known as "cognitive dissonance," which is very much at work here.

Cognitive dissonance is our tendency or need to justify a decision that we have made, or something that we have done. In this case, our relocation. In our attempt to justify our move we unconsciously focus on every positive aspect of it, and every aspect that is likeable about life in the new country. This causes us to ignore anything that may be perceived as negative. Much of our euphoric state of mind is a result of this psychological mechanism. However, please note—it doesn't last long!

> The honeymoon is a pleasing and happy phase, but it is also an intensive learning period.

Learning a new language, adopting a different dress code, eating unfamiliar food, and learning different customs and etiquette are all part of the excitement and challenge of moving to a new country. Newcomers fairly quickly assimilate a great deal of knowledge and develop basic skills to enable them to function on a daily basis. They often study the local language with zeal, and most make considerable progress.

During this time there may be pressing issues to deal with, such as renting a home, arranging utilities, buying a car, opening a bank account, and finding schools. Some people achieve these early tasks successfully, and feel an accompanying sense of accomplishment. Even if they encounter some stumbling blocks, these are all part of the novelty. Each small victory makes them feel that they are making the transition successfully.

However, for others, as soon as they begin to tackle these arrangements, and as soon as problems arise, the euphoria of the honeymoon phase comes to an end, and they start to experience the slump of the culture-shock phase.

The excitement of the honeymoon phase often subsides after a few days, or a few weeks. In some lucky cases it may last for months, or even years.

Some people don't experience a honeymoon phase at all, and move straight into the culture-shock phase.

What is important to understand is that, despite its euphoric nature, the honeymoon phase marks the beginning of the cross-cultural adaptation process, and therefore it is a period where much is being learned. It is also the phase in which culture shock is triggered and begins to "breed" as a result of change overload. Thus, this is a critical period in which to take the essential steps that will enable you to prevent or minimize the impact of culture shock.

Chapter 15

SETTLING IN

This is the time to rearrange the details and reestablish the routines of your life, to familiarize yourself and engage with your new environment, and, importantly, to build up your capacity and confidence to navigate your new surroundings.

This phase is about re-learning the small tasks of everyday life. It involves all the basic "how-to" details—how to get from home to work, how to find your way to school, how to find an Internet provider, where to shop, how to pay on the bus, and many other details.

In spite of its euphoric aura, the settling-in period is a time where moments are lived intensely. It is a frantic and bewildering period that is both physically and psychologically taxing. You may find yourself tested to your limits.

> The most important advice to travelers is: *Be patient!* Expect setbacks, errors, and annoyance. With or without support, you are likely to experience some degree of frustration during the settling-in period.

Everyone has to deal with unforeseen obstacles, delays, and other occurrences that may be annoying, frustrating, and, at times, costly.

> *"What makes a difference to your settling-in period is not what happens, but what you make of it."*
> Anthony Robbins

What makes the difference is your reaction, the meaning you attach to these events, and the way you deal with them when they occur. This will make or break your entire relocation experience. What matters is your resilience and attitude, rather than what setbacks and obstacles you face.

SIX ESSENTIAL ELEMENTS FOR SUCCESSFUL SETTLING IN

+ Putting yourself and your family first.
+ Creating a welcoming home base.
+ Establishing a pleasant and relaxed routine.
+ Having a comfortably paced settling-in plan to work to.
+ Taking time to explore and master your new surroundings gradually.
+ Establishing new ties and a support system.

PUT YOURSELF AND YOUR FAMILY FIRST!

As you plunge, exhausted and bewildered, into a foreign country, you will find yourself spending much more time together with your family than you did before, in an environment that may put a strain on your relationships. You may have to rely on each other much more than before, simply because there is no one else around to support you.

Many people report that relocating abroad has had a "magnifying-glass" effect on their relationships. Indeed, the challenges of relocation can put relationships to the test. They can improve strong relationships, while struggling ones may deteriorate further. All the moods and emotions provoked by the move will eventually land on the family table in the form of arguments, complaints, hurt feelings, harsh words, and sour moods. It is unrealistic to expect that moving abroad will solve marital or family problems. The likelihood is that it will make them worse. Thus, if you have unresolved family issues, work on them before your move.

> Put yourself and your family first! Forget the suitcases and scattered boxes, the mess, your work, the paperwork, or anything else that is on your mind. Look after your family's well-being and emotional needs, and your relationships.

Some tips to guide you through this period

✦ Keep the communication channels open, and speak up. If you can communicate well, share frustrations and difficulties, and support each other as you face and handle the challenges of your new environment, your relationships will grow stronger and closer. Try not to bottle up negative feelings. Acknowledge them as normal.

✦ Teamwork, togetherness, and mutual support will aid your family's adaptation process. Feeling abandoned will hinder it. Therefore, if you are employed, try to avoid separating from your family during the first days.

✦ When attending to your settling-in arrangements, find an enjoyable activity to occupy the children. Don't drag them around with you or make them wait in the car while you are running errands.

✦ Each member of the family is likely to experience the challenges of your move in a different way and at different times. If you have young children, you may have to take on the role of shock absorber, making sure that everyone's needs are met.

✦ Make a conscious effort to establish a comfortable home base, even if you are in temporary lodgings (see page 139).

✦ Establish a temporary family routine as soon as possible (see page 141).

✦ Many families find themselves separated for months during the transition period. Some overseas jobs also require extensive travel. This leaves the accompanying spouse with the task of running the family's everyday life on his or her own. If this is your situation, it is vital that you quickly build a support network around your spouse and family.

✦ Another known phenomenon is that the trailing spouse often finds it harder to adapt than the employed spouse, especially if he or she is a parent and unemployed. Furthermore, in a new environment, the working spouse may get caught up in new separate activities and spend less time with the family. Communicating and negotiating "together time" and establishing a support network can alleviate some of these stressors.

✦ Roles may change within the relationship. An accompanying spouse who has given up work and income may feel uncomfortable with the new economic dependency. Take time to discuss this change and establish an agreement on how money issues will be dealt with.

✦ The working spouse, on the other hand, may find the new responsibility for the family income and well-being a burden.

✦ Stuck with the kids in an emply home? Being stuck with young children in temporary housing or an empty home for a long period is undoubtedly one of the most common nightmares of international relocation, and you can expect boredom, anger, and frustration. Here is what you can do:
  • Be mindful that your children need the assurance of your presence. Spend quality time with them.
  • Find simple games and ways to keep them occupied.
  • Take time to explore your new location with them.
  • Involve them in unpacking suitcases, setting up their room, and shopping.
  • Give them simple chores that they can do with you.

✦ Children are likely to become over-stimulated and experience strong emotional reactions when taken away from their familiar environment. They may become more immature in their behavior, may be fearful, clingy, and whiny, and may at times become hyperactive or withdrawn. Prepare yourself in advance for these changes in behavior.

- Offer more physical closeness.
- Talk and listen to your children.
- Do things together. Arrange fun outings, especially during the first days.
- Be especially calm and understanding about accidents such as bedwetting.
- Don't change your level of discipline. Keep to your usual standards. This is not a good time to become a disciplinarian, even if the kids are getting on your nerves.
- Establish a routine as quickly as you can. Even a temporary routine will make life more predictable and secure for you and your children.

✦ As you confront the strangeness of the new place, you may find yourself becoming homesick, and missing family, friends, and places.

- Allow yourself to grieve for these losses.
- Communicate with people back home regularly.
- Think of small comfort items that you can get, or routines that you can do, that will help you feel content and will satisfy your need for security.

CREATING A WELCOMING HOME BASE

Your first home away from home may well be a hotel room, a room at your relatives' home, a temporary apartment, or your permanent place. Whatever your home is, it plays an essential role in the settling-in period. It becomes your comfort zone—the place where you can retreat from the demands and stresses of the world outside, unwind, and recharge.

Your priority on arrival is to set it up as soon as possible and make it welcoming and comfortable. Even if you have little control over your environment, small items can make all the difference.

Invite friends or colleagues to visit you in your home as soon as possible, even if you are in a temporary place, with just the bare necessities. Having guests over will give you a reason to brighten things up and create a sense of home. Don't wait until you have a perfect place.

The following is one of the simplest, yet most powerful strategies for restoring your sense of comfort and well-being.

> Make arrangements for transition times,
> and make them as comfortable as possible.
> Take care of details. Small things are important
> at this point. Find the items or habits that
> make you feel good, and stick to them amid the change.

We all have little "comfort items" in our lives that make us feel content and happy. Young children often have a favorite toy, or blanket, or drink, and we all know children who simply can't leave home or go to bed without their comfort item. This is true for adults, too. These items may be a type of food or drink, a book or a newspaper, a type of music, a piece of jewelry, an item of clothing, a diary, or anything else.

Comforts can also be habits, such as grooming or make-up routines, having morning tea or coffee, reading in bed before going to sleep, or exercise routines.

This strategy acknowledges that during turbulent transition times many of the comfort items that we normally have within easy reach are not available to us. Several, if not all, of our routines and habits are interrupted. What we can do to restore our sense of comfort and security is to make arrangements for these times, and make them as comfortable as possible, by ensuring that we have within our reach just a few comfort items that will make us feel content, secure, and relaxed, and by sticking to a few small routines or habits in the course of the change.

The Value of Chocolate

In one of my workshops, one of the participants challenged my "comfort items" strategy.

He exclaimed, "My home is all packed in boxes, I am about to make the biggest change of my life, and you are trying to tell me that what I need to

*think about while my life is in chaos is how to get the chocolate that my wife
likes, and my special brand of ice cream?"*

*My simple answer is, "Yes!" This is a tried and tested strategy, and it works.
Try it yourself, and see how those little comfort items make a difference.*

THE ARRIVAL OF THE SHIPMENT

Often the shipment arrives when your morale is low, and,
although it can cheer you up, the mess involved in unpacking
can derail your spirit even further.

+ Don't let the shippers just pile up things anywhere on
  the floor. Plan in advance where you want the bigger
  items to go, and show the movers where to put them.
+ Use an empty room, or a corner, or a garage to store the
  boxes, and unpack a few every day. This "warehouse
  method" avoids having boxes scattered all over the house.
+ Children of all ages enjoy unpacking and rediscovering
  their own items and arranging their rooms. Let them
  be involved!

ESTABLISHING A COMFORTABLE FAMILY ROUTINE

One of our basic human needs is security. Our sense of
security develops by living in an environment that is known,
comfortable, and predictable, and by having stability in our
lives, which includes following certain routines and habits. Our
familiar and habitual life setting is, in fact, our comfort zone.

However, when we relocate, particularly during the settling-
in period, all or most of our comforting routines and familiar
items are taken away, and we find ourselves constantly
functioning outside our comfort zone.

> When you arrive, consciously create structure
> and predictability in your life by establishing routines
> that will make you feel secure and in control.
> Stick to them amid the change.

This strategy is specifically designed to alleviate the challenges of transitional periods. It suggests that you make a conscious effort to make these early days as predictable, regular, and manageable as possible. Create temporary routines that will help you to feel secure and in control, and stick to them during this period.

These routines can be small and trivial, such as having a family dinner every day, playing with the children at the same time every day, taking a walk or exercising at the same times, or speaking with a family member on specific days and times.

Each and every small routine becomes an anchor that introduces structure and predictability into our chaotic lives, helping us to feel more comfortable, secure, and confident, despite the instability around us.

This strategy is vital if you are relocating with children. Children need structure and order in their lives to feel secure and content. Thus, it is essential to create both routines and guidelines for them during those periods of transition, and ensure they understand and follow them.

MANAGING YOUR SETTLING-IN PROCESS

Many people may be eager, soon after arrival, to engage with, explore, and discover their new environment. Others may be impatient to get the settling-in arrangements out of the way. As a result of these two impulses, many people throw themselves into a variety of activities, which may cause physical or psychological overload. It is wiser to monitor and pace yourself slowly. Balance is critical at this point.

Striking a Balance

The central principle to guide you during the settling-in period is "balance" between five types of activity:
+ Carrying out your settling-in arrangements.
+ Taking time to relax and recuperate.
+ Spending time with your family.
+ Exploring your new environment.
+ Taking time to have fun.

Balancing these activities will enable you to carry out your settling-in arrangements in an orderly manner, and, at the same time, will give you the time you need to relax, be with your family, and enjoy and appreciate your new life and what it can offer you. Maintaining balance during this period is extremely important to keep your spirits up, and to help you retain your sense of enthusiasm, adventure, and curiosity for longer. Don't bury your enthusiasm by doing too much too soon, or by focusing only on your settling-in arrangements.

Managing Your Settling-In Tasks
- ✦ List all your settling-in tasks.
- ✦ Prioritize your list.
- ✦ Decide what you will focus on in the coming week.
- ✦ Break down bigger tasks into smaller steps.
- ✦ Schedule these steps into your planner.
- ✦ Take action! Follow your plan.
- ✦ Work on and attempt to complete just one task each day. When you complete this task, proceed to the next.

What are your plans, then? What do you plan to accomplish during the first weeks of your relocation? The following exercise is designed to help you think about and plan your first days and weeks in your new country.

✍ PLANNING YOUR SETTLING-IN ARRANGEMENTS
1. List your settling-in arrangements and tasks here:

Main tasks	Due Date
Legal	
Housing	
Work	
Finances / banking	
Education / language learning	
Health	
Communication	
Transportation	
Social / networks	
The shipment	

2. Prioritize. Which items on your list need to be carried out first? Put them in order.

_____
_____
_____
_____
_____
_____
_____
_____

3. Schedule all the tasks in your planner. Ensure you leave enough time every day and on weekends to enjoy leisure activities, rest, and spend time with your family.

4. What pleasurable things would you like to do during the first weeks of your stay?

_____
_____
_____
_____

5. How would you like to spend family time during the next weeks?

_____
_____
_____
_____

6. Now, schedule these leisure events into your planner. If you have followed the previous steps, you should now have a timed plan made up of daily task lists. The next step is to act on it!

London's Famous "Catch 22" Situation
Daniel's Story

I came on my own to find a house in June, and Dora and the kids joined me in July. I went to a realtor, and he drove me around, and after seeing a few houses, I decided to rent one of them. When I wanted to make the down payment with my international Visa card, he says, "I can't accept that; do you have a local credit card or check?"

I said, "No, not yet, I haven't opened a bank account." He says, "Well, then, open a bank account first, and then come back to me to finalize the contract."

So, I go to the bank, I stand in line patiently, and when I finally get to the desk she smiles, gets the forms for me, and explains how to fill them. "We will also need a proof of your address," she says, "an electricity bill would be fine."

"But we don't have an address yet," I say. "We have just arrived, and although I found a house, I have not yet finalized the contract, and I don't have a bill to show you." "No problem, your rental contract will be fine as a proof of your address," she says, and smiles politely.

But I am a little angry now. So I say, slowly and loudly, "I do not have an address here because the agent wants me to have a local bank account first."

She gives me a funny look, and says, "I am so sorry, sir, you can't open a bank account without a local permanent address."

I really didn't know what to do! I had such a bad headache I decided to go back to my B&B, have a rest, and think it through.

Luckily, the B&B owners were there. They were originally from India, and had been living here for more than twenty years. I told them what had happened, and they laughed and said, "That's the famous London Catch-22 situation you've got locked into! Let's see how we can get you out of this."

They called a friend of theirs who was a realtor, and took me to his office. The realtor said, "Don't worry, you can pay with your international credit card here. But first let's find a house for you." So I saw a few more houses, chose one, and made the down payment on my card. The realtor then gave me a letter for the bank, and even went with me to ensure that it all went smoothly.

*I remember being so frustrated and angry over this. I simply could not believe that this * * * * could happen in London!*

LEARNING TO MASTER YOUR NEW ENVIRONMENT

We often take for granted our ability to manage and function in our own environment. We shop, cook, use a washing machine, drive, take a bus, and use a telephone or ATM on a daily basis without much thought.

When we relocate to a new place, the level of knowledge required to accomplish these tasks soon becomes apparent. We won't know where things are, or how things work, even in our own home. And this state of being unable to function in our environment ruptures our sense of mastery. We may feel helpless, confused, and incompetent.

Some tips to help you acquaint yourself with your environment and master it quickly:

✦ Take time first to learn how to operate all the equipment in your new home. If, like many of us, you avoid reading manuals, ask someone to show you. Being able to run your own home is vital to your sense of security and confidence.

✦ Explore your nearest vicinity. Even if you are in temporary lodgings, take time to look around and get a sense of distances and directions. Note the amenities and services available locally, and transportation routes.

✦ Find out where your nearest hospital is located and what to do in an emergency.

✦ Where available, take a tourist bus ride around the city. Otherwise, just take a bus to the end of the line, or hire a driver or tour guide for a day.

✦ Invest in a tourist guidebook (which it would be better to buy in your homeland) and a good map of the city.

✦ Ask your mentor to show you around and take you to the nearest shopping and leisure areas.

✦ On arrival, you may have a lot of "how" and "where" questions on your mind. How do I open a bank account? Where are the local schools? How do I register my children for school? How do we register with a doctor and dentist? How do we apply for services, such as gas, electricity, water, and a phone line? How do we find an Internet provider? List all your questions, and ask around to get clear answers. Don't put yourself through the torture of figuring out all these small details yourself. Ask your mentor or a colleague for advice. A few trips with an experienced expatriate or emigrant after you arrive will reveal information that would have taken you months to find out on your own.

✦ When shopping, you may find that stores, products, and labels are different from what you are used to. In some countries the whole system is organized differently; in some cultures bargaining is expected for the most basic items; in other places you order and pay, then present your receipt to receive your purchases.

✦ Many of the recipes you brought from home may be unsuitable for your new country. Key ingredients may be unavailable, different units of measurement may be used, and the taste of ingredients may be different. Ask your fellow countrymen about substitutes, and get food preparation advice from experienced travelers.

"WE CAN'T GET THAT HERE"

During the first months abroad, you will start to accumulate a list of things that "they don't have here," "we can't get here," and "we can't do here."

These may be certain foods or drinks, or a particular spice, a replacement part for a gadget you have brought with you, a service, an appliance, a newspaper, a radio station, a type of art, music, or clothing, or amenities for a sport or hobby.

Learning to get by without these small things requires us to make scores of little adjustments. While most people cope well enough by finding substitutes, or importing things from home, the sheer annoyance and inconvenience of trying to do without some items can wear you down. (See Chapter 4 for ways to resolve this situation.)

ESTABLISHING NEW TIES AND A SUPPORT SYSTEM
Having a support system, especially during the settling-in period, is an effective way to counter culture shock. It is therefore essential that you begin to network as soon as you arrive, and help your family, especially children and teens, to build their new social circles.

Research on immigrants and expatriates suggests that most newcomers tend to gravitate toward their own countrymen during their first period abroad, and that those who enjoy the support of their compatriots during this period experience a softer landing, and have an easier adaptation process, than those who don't have this type of support.

Some immigrant and expatriate communities are well organized to provide considerable assistance to newcomers, including providing information, practical and emotional support, cultural orientation, language support, and networking opportunities. In my experience, however, even a small community with just a few families can provide some form of support. I have found that the kindness and willingness of veteran fellow countrymen to help and pitch in with information, advice, and practical help can be one of the most delightful aspects of relocation.

Some tips to guide you through your networking
✦ An important first step is to locate medical professionals who can speak your language. Your embassy or expatriate community may be able to help you. Establish a connection with these health professionals, visit their clinics, and register before you need them.
✦ If you are employed, your colleagues and their spouses may be a good source of information and support. Often a colleague may be assigned to help you settle in.
✦ To find fellow countrymen, start with the embassy, and then search for religious or ethnic organizations, as well as forums and Web sites on the Internet. Look in the local newspapers, local language schools, charities, playgroups, coffee shops, and classes and clubs where your countrymen are likely to congregate.

✦ Beware of people with negative attitudes who are eager to spread the gloom to newcomers to justify their own experiences!

✦ We all gravitate toward people with whom we have something in common—it does not necessarily have to be language and culture. A particular profession, hobby, or interest, may be a good common ground to look for.

✦ Try to make friends with a variety of people in your new country—both your own countrymen and locals.

✦ If you find yourself isolated, be more creative in developing your support network.

✦ Don't confine yourself to virtual contacts such as people you chat to on the Internet. Make regular efforts to socialize. Go out, visit others, and invite them over as soon as possible. Don't wait until your home is in a perfect state.

✦ Networking is an important skill. Develop it so that you can effectively use any professional or social event to establish new relationships.

✦ In some countries, local people may be eager to befriend you. In others, it may be more difficult to make local friends. Beside the language and cultural barriers, local people are immersed in their own lives, and surrounded by their friends and families, and they may not feel they have the time or patience to establish new friendships. Respect this state, and don't become upset about it. Get advice from veterans about how to establish connections with locals.

✦ Beware of local people who may be too eager to meet you. Especially in poor countries, they may be seeking financial assistance or help in getting a visa to your country. If a relationship makes you uncomfortable, don't maintain it.

✦ Prepare in advance for holidays. Consider going home to celebrate with family members, or inviting them over. Alternatively, get your fellow countrymen together to help you keep home traditions alive.

THE LURE OF THE EMIGRANT COMMUNITY

A word of warning about the ties you establish with people from your homeland.

During the initial period of arrival, the lure of the expatriate or emigrant community can be almost irresistible.

These communities serve a legitimate and essential need to break away from the relentless demands of the new environment, and can, at this point in your journey, function as a safe haven for you and your family. They can provide both practical help and emotional support, and as mentioned above, this type of support can alleviate many of the settling-in difficulties.

However, in the long run, this network can become a trap that slows down and even hampers your integration into the local community and culture. In a sense, it enables you to live abroad without ever leaving your own cultural comfort zone.

It is also important to be aware that expatriate communities are very transient in their nature. Veteran residents return every year, and new expatriates arrive.

Living within the confines of the expatriate bubble means that you and your family will be going through a continuous series of beginnings and farewells during your entire stay. Most people, and especially children, find this lack of stability in their social circle unsettling.

Thus, do enjoy the support they can offer you upon arrival, but leave your mental door open to establishing ties outside this confined circle.

Chapter 16

THE CHALLENGES OF THE SETTLING-IN PERIOD

Before you can integrate with the local people and adapt to their culture, you must first survive the move! Undoubtedly, the main challenge of the settling-in period is culture shock, which is discussed in detail in Part 5. However, the first stage of relocation involves getting used to the country and the stresses of managing the many details that will make up your new life: the setting up of your new home and routines. These challenges often provoke a "transition shock," which is often considered as the first phase of culture shock (the disorientation phase).

> Transition shock is caused by change overload, resulting from the commotion and disorder that newcomers experience during the settling-in period and the discomfort that comes from the unfamiliarity of everything.

Newcomers often experience constant stress, confusion, and disorientation caused by the sheer quantity of things that need to be learned and done at this point, and by uncertainty about how to go about them in the new place.

The good news about these settling-in trials is that, unlike cultural adjustments, most of us have experienced them in the normal course of our lives—when moving house, changing jobs, going to college, and on other occasions, and therefore we can draw on our past experience to alleviate them.

The problem is that the settling-in adjustment and the cultural adaptation occur at the same time, competing for our attention and depleting our reservoir of energy. So it's important to recognize that the settling-in adjustments impinge on the pace and the outcome of our cultural learning and adaptation process.

The impact of the settling-in challenges can be so critical and direct that if we don't recognize and attend to them the resulting stress and anxiety can overwhelm and defeat us to the point that we may be experiencing a "crash landing" (see page 159). The strange thing about crash landing is that it has all the signs and symptoms of culture shock, yet it happens before we have had a chance to become acquainted with and experience the local culture.

Some people experience the disorientation phase in parallel to the honeymoon phase. However, when these phases occur at the same time, the sense of confusion and disorientation can be veiled and, therefore, ignored, due to the euphoria of the honeymoon phase.

The main challenges of the settling-in period are the loss of the automatic pilot and the unfamiliarity of everything. The main difficulty they pose is change overload and a loss of confidence, which are the chief causes of the culture-shock experience.

THE LOSS OF THE "AUTOMATIC PILOT"

During the first weeks and sometimes months of relocation, you are likely to lose your automatic pilot in some areas of life. Soon after you arrive you may notice that you have to give your full attention to, and invest conscious mental effort in actions that you used to perform automatically in your homeland.

For the first few days nothing is going to be automatic. Your first breakfast, your first bath, driving, shopping, paying a bill, even walking around the block: everything you do will require more mental attention than it would if you were doing it at home. This means that the time and energy that would have been available for more sophisticated tasks now goes into those very basic coping and survival functions. As a result, the more complicated functions are set aside and are likely to take much longer to accomplish.

The main problem is that until these things become automatic again we are likely to have a very low opinion of ourselves. We think, "If something this simple is so difficult, what am I going to do about something really complicated?" The tendency with most people is to become frustrated about the simple things that need to be re-learned, as well as to get upset about the higher-order actions that don't get done at all, or are done at a much slower pace than usual. A common complaint is, "Everything is so slow here!"

For most people, strange as this may sound, the loss of the automatic pilot and this state of "lower functionality" really hits them at their core. This is because we expect to learn new things in our new place, but we don't expect to have to re-learn the things that we normally do automatically. As a result of this, little things can become a significant source of frustration and distress. Newcomers often feel that they have lost control over their lives. They may feel inadequate or vulnerable, and experience a slump in confidence and self-esteem. When things on their "to do" list are suspended or interrupted, they become frustrated, upset, and angry. And it is this state that triggers the culture-shock downfall. It is important, therefore, to address and handle this situation effectively. (See how on page 158.)

THE UNFAMILIARITY OF EVERYTHING

Another feature of this early phase of adaptation, and probably the most unsettling, is the newness and unfamiliarity of everything: having to face an environment in which we don't know where or how to do the simplest things.

In the months following your relocation, you will be interacting, day in and day out, with people you don't know well, in a language you are still not very comfortable with, in places that you have never been to before. You will be operating machines and devices you are not familiar with, having to attend to details you are not aware of, and participating in events that you do not recognize the etiquette of, and then coming back to a home that doesn't feel like home.

Obviously, we all do this on a smaller scale when we go abroad on vacation, or change workplaces, or move to a new neighborhood. But it does take more energy and effort to interact with unfamiliar people in an unfamiliar environment than to interact with people you know in a known environment.

The problem with functioning in a foreign environment is that we cannot really loosen up. We have to be constantly on our guard, and monitor what is going on around us as well as our own behavior. This takes considerable mental effort. The upshot is that after a few hours in an unfamiliar environment we experience over-stimulation, which results in mental and physical fatigue, and a loss of self-control.

Consequently, most people experience a sense of restlessness, irritability, and incompetence. And when we are exhausted, our normal self-control and patience levels go down, and we are more likely to fall out with the people around us—our friends and family—over petty things. We might become disproportionately angry and depressed when they don't understand us, or don't give us the support or space we need.

Small problems—delays, incomplete projects, unsatisfactory results—may make us feel discontented and, at times, frustrated with the way we have handled things. We may feel impatient about the way things are done in our new country, and at the same time have a sense of inadequacy because of our inability to manage or direct the events and situations that occur. Many travelers become anxious, and begin to wonder whether they can cope with the new situation.

Help! How Do I Pay the Bus Fare?
Lily's Story

"I remember my first days in Munich. One of the difficult moments I had was when I wanted to get a bus from the central station to the university. I had a bus map, and the man in the tourist information office showed me where to find the station, and told me which bus to take. What he didn't tell me was how to pay for the bus, and it just didn't occur to me to ask him.

When I got to the station, I realized that people were holding some kind of ticket. I didn't know where to get one, and I became very anxious. I asked the lady in front of me about it, but she couldn't understand what I was saying. Then a bus came, they all got on it, and I was on my own at the station. I was almost in tears.

Twenty minutes later, my bus arrived. I climbed up and asked: "How much?" but the irritated driver just opened the door and pointed to a machine on the other side of the road. I felt like a naughty child being sent to her room. I got down, sat down on the pavement, and cried.

Luckily, some students came out of a nearby bar. They went with me to the ticket machine, showed me how to operate it, and waited with me for the next bus. One of them even got on the bus with me to show me how to insert the ticket into the machine.

I felt so stupid and vulnerable. All I wanted to do was to go to my room. For the next three months, I barely left the campus area."

CHANGE OVERLOAD

It is intuitively apparent that too much change will put a strain on people. Two of our most basic human needs are to be secure and to have some control over our lives, our circumstances, and our environment. Our sense of security and control develops by acquiring skills that enable us to affect and master significant aspects of our lives, and by creating stability and predictability in our lives.

But during an international move, and specifically during the settling-in period, everything changes at once. The unfamiliar environment relentlessly assaults our senses with constant stimuli. There are no comforting routines or familiar things in our surroundings. Everything takes mental effort to figure out, and our most basic skills are put to the test. As a result, our sense of mastery and security is shaken.

The first emotional reaction provoked by change overload is alertness. This is a neutral state, which can develop into a positive state, such as curiosity, eagerness, and anticipation, or into a negative state, such as disorientation, stress, and panic.

The problem is that the longer the state of alertness is sustained the more likely it is that we will become over-stimulated. Our attentiveness will deteriorate, and fatigue will set in. This may, in turn, provoke intense emotional reactions: we are likely to feel overwhelmed, powerless, and anxious. Our natural instinct will be to withdraw from the environment that assaults our senses.

THE LOSS OF SELF-CONFIDENCE

A cross-cultural move can be a heavy blow to your ego. At first, you will not know how to get around, ask for directions, or find out where to eat. You may find yourself stumbling over cultural and language mistakes that a six-year-old local child wouldn't make.

Everything will go at a much slower pace than you are used to, which is very frustrating for someone who is used to getting quick results. You may find yourself dependent on other people to do the simplest things—even making a phone call or doing the shopping. Incomprehensible local rules may limit your activities. The sense of belonging and comfort you have taken for granted is nowhere to be found.

Many people experience a loss of control over their lives. They may feel incompetent, helpless, and defenseless—"like a child." The stress and gloomy mood, in turn, can deplete their energy levels. The result is a severe and abrupt drop in their self-confidence.

They may doubt their decision to relocate, which may bring their settling-in and adaptation process to a halt. For many people this is the first slump toward culture-shock depression.

To prevent this state and minimize its impact, follow the tips and tools offered below.

How to Address These Challenges

✦ First: be aware of these challenges. Awareness will heighten your resilience. Once you realize that it will take time to learn the basic aspects of life, then you won't be taken by surprise, and you won't get upset.

✦ Give yourself more time to learn how to do all those ordinary little things, and to familiarize yourself with the people around you and your new environment. Be patient. You are, after all, a newcomer, and you are at the point where your learning curve is the steepest. Not knowing how to do things is legitimate.

✦ Rest assured that you will regain your automatic pilot capacities very soon. Most people recover most of their automatic pilot functions in two to four weeks.

✦ Consciously take time to learn these details. Be proactive, and ask for instructions. Ask a friend or mentor to provide information and clarify how things work. The more control you gain over your environment, the better you will feel.

✦ Structure your learning and pace yourself. Familiarize yourself with your surroundings gradually. Focus on mastering one thing at a time, and when you have done that, go to the next. For example, take time to acquaint yourself with all the equipment in your home, and only when you feel competent in this environment, move on to the next challenge.

✦ Create a comfort zone where you feel confident and in control; an area into which you can withdraw, unwind, and recharge. Take time to personalize this area.

✦ Spend time with people you know well and are comfortable with on a regular basis. This will help to restore your confidence and allow you to be in an environment that is comforting, and that does not demand so much effort.

✦ Make arrangements for these special times, and make them as comfortable and pleasant as possible (see page 139).
✦ Balance between withdrawal and exploration. Beware of becoming over-stimulated.
✦ Take care of details. Small habits are very important at this point. Find the small items or habits that make you feel good, and claim them (see page 140).
✦ Create temporary routines that make you feel comfortable and in control, and stick to these routines amid the changes (see page 141).
✦ Review your learning to help yourself to absorb the new information. A good way to do this is to write down every night what you have learned that day, or to share your new knowledge with someone else. Writing a relocation journal can be very useful as a way of reviewing your new learning.

CRASH LANDING
Some people are so overwhelmed on arrival in their new country that they dive straight into the culture-shock phase, and all they want to do is to jump on the next plane home!

Depressing poverty, in-your-face beggars, alarming traffic, noise, overcrowding, pollution, crime, hostile stares, unfamiliar animals and insects, and many other unfamiliar sights, sounds, and smells may assault our senses.

The time zone and climate may be different. The rhythm of daily life is unfamiliar. We may face a new job—or no job. Our home doesn't feel like home. The habits of people around us may seem strange, or even frightening. Nothing is obvious, and everything is a challenge to figure out.

We become over-stimulated. This often provokes an intense emotional reaction. We may feel overwhelmed, constantly stressed, and irritable, and desperately seek to withdraw from this relentless attack on our senses.

Our natural instinct will be to protect our family—and this may override any concern for career, study, or any other goal we have set ourselves to achieve.

Problems such as illness, injury, theft, items lost on arrival, poor or substandard lodging or transportation, financial issues, lack of communication with people back home, or conflicts with family members can increase the chances of a crash landing.

Risk Factors for Having a Crash Landing
✦ Being a first-time traveler, without the experience of moving.
✦ Moving from a very safe, structured, and familiar environment to a chaotic, dangerous, or hectic one.
✦ The new culture is radically different from our own.
✦ Not speaking the language.
✦ Unrealistic expectations that crash in the face of reality.
✦ Moving on our own, or with people we are not comfortable with.
✦ Arriving physically or emotionally drained.
✦ Having no support system in the destination country.
✦ Relocating reluctantly, or being "dragged along behind."
✦ Going through a major life change, such as divorce or retirement, at the same time.
✦ Poor planning or preparation, leading to chaotic first days.
✦ Having to deal with unexpected or severe adversity, such as illness, injury, or crime, on arrival.

How to Handle and Ease a Crash Landing
✦ Take steps to increase your comfort and security: ensure you have a few comfort items that will make you feel content, secure, and relaxed.
✦ Establish a comfortable daily routine as quickly as you can.
✦ Focus on the enjoyable things the country has to offer.
✦ Seek companionship: spend time with others from your homeland.
✦ Ask a relative to come and stay with you for a while.

✦ If you feel uncomfortable at home, find a place where you can relax or "be yourself" at least for a few hours a day.

✦ Don't make a hasty decision to return home. Give yourself a fixed period to decide whether to stay or leave.

✦ Practice stress-reducing techniques such as sports, yoga, listening to relaxing music, or meditation.

WHEN FRUSTRATION SETS IN

✦ If things go wrong and frustration sets in, speak up, state the problem, and find a solution. Don't pile up unspoken complaints!

✦ Make a list of everything you find frustrating. Choose one issue that you wish to handle and focus on that until it is settled and completed to your satisfaction. Then move to the next item on your list.

✦ Keep telling yourself that you can succeed, and that you will make it through the rough times. Others have managed it, and so will you!

✦ Don't be hard on yourself or on your spouse or children.

✦ Use your sense of humor to relieve tension and frustration.

> An additional area of unfamiliarity that newcomers often come to grips with at this point is the cultural aspect.

Newcomers may now realize that there are endless subtle cultural differences that leave them facing a multitude of puzzling issues. Many of these probably did not concern them at home. But here they may find that they have to give them conscious attention: things like how to address and greet people, what to wear to work or to a party, how to conduct themselves in a meeting, what they can discuss in different situations, and many more.

Furthermore, their language skills might not serve them as well as expected. They might not be able to convey their needs or communicate requests correctly, and as a result, their capacity to progress with their plans and arrangements may be hampered. All of these issues can exhaust the newcomer's reservoir of energy, self-control, and sense of humor.

Some people report that during this phase even doing the laundry can become a significant effort, and that making a phone call can bring about an emotional crisis.

An important point to understand here is that the disorientation phase is where the downturn in the newcomer's psychological state begins to occur and where culture shock is triggered. Therefore, if you can manage this phase well, you can prevent and significantly moderate the symptoms of the following stages.

Chapter 17

CULTURE SHOCK: THE CHALLENGE OF CHANGE

Imagine the following familiar scenario.

*You have just arrived at your vacation destination with your
wife and children. This is a country you have never visited
before, and you can't speak the language, but you are hoping
you can get by with English. You are excited and looking forward
to a fantastic week in the sun. However, there are some small
things that don't go as smoothly as you might have hoped.*

*To start with, your flight has been delayed. You arrive at the
local airport at 2:00 a.m. The car rental office is closed, and you
can't collect the car you have ordered and already paid for. Also,
you need cash. After a long search for a cash machine, you find
one, but the instructions aren't in English, and there's nowhere
else to change money.*

*You get a taxi to the hotel. The driver doesn't turn on the
meter. You try to ask him about it, but he doesn't seem to
understand you. You sit there, irritated and worried about the
cost of the journey. When you arrive at your destination, the
driver asks you to pay what seems an outrageous sum. You feel a
fool, but, being unable to communicate with him, you grudgingly
pay. You don't tip him, and your wife gives you a nasty look
(meaning "stingy!").*

At the hotel, the porter insists on carrying your bags. You haven't got any change, so you give him a dollar instead of local currency. Your wife gives you that look again.

In the room, it takes you ten minutes to figure out how the shower works. By the time you manage to operate it, you are wet, so is the floor, and the children are asleep.

A few hours later, the children wake up complaining that they are cold. You try to turn off the air-conditioning, but after pushing every button on the remote control you give up and go down to reception to ask them to send someone to your room to show you how. You don't even try to use the phone, because at this point you don't have the patience to read the phone instruction booklet.

Finally, you fall asleep—exhausted, irritated, impatient, and worried.

Many of us can probably relate to this story. Not a great start to a vacation, is it? Some hints of culture shock surface here.

Obviously, even when we are abroad only for a brief vacation, some form of cross-cultural adaptation is essential for us to be able to carry out simple everyday tasks or activities. To cushion our landing, and to ensure an enjoyable and fruitful relocation experience, some practical and psychological preparation is vital.

You may be asking yourself, "What is the significance of culture shock? Why should I take the time to study and prepare for it?" In my experience, your ability to manage and cope with culture shock can make or break your relocation journey. And, as I have seen many times in my line of work, the cost of culture shock can be staggering.

According to a survey (GMAC Global Relocation Services) published in 2006, 34 percent of expatriates fail to complete their assignments, either returning prematurely to their homelands or leaving the company. Further surveys (Brookfield Global Relocation Trends) conducted between 2007 and 2010 repeatedly reveal that the main cause of expatriate assignment failure is the inability of the expatriate and his or her family to cope with the challenges of adaptation, and the ensuing culture shock.

The costs of relocation failure are well documented. For the people involved, there are high personal, career, and family costs, as well as time, effort, and financial losses. There are often detrimental psychological consequences, which can lead to family breakups and health problems. The organizational costs of failed relocation assignments are also very high. They range from incomplete or abandoned assignments to loss of effort, time, money, business, clientele, and reputation.

The next chapters will provide you with essential information on culture shock: what it is, why it occurs, what triggers it, what its phases and symptoms are, and how to moderate and alleviate the symptoms. Though these chapters may not be pleasant to read, they will provide you with the ability to foresee what lies ahead, and will help you to build a solid foundation from which you can take action with confidence and determination.

> ### *WHAT IS CULTURE SHOCK?*
> Culture shock is the initial psychological response to displacement. It occurs when we move from a known environment to an unfamiliar setting in which we are unable to make sense of events and function at our usual level.

The term "culture shock" was coined by the anthropologist Dr. Kalervo Oberg in the 1950s to describe the psychological upheaval experienced when we move from a known environment to an unfamiliar setting, in which we are unable to make sense of events and function at our usual level.

> ### WHAT ARE THE SYMPTOMS
> ### OF CULTURE SHOCK?
> The effects may range from mild uneasiness,nervousness,
> fatigue, or lonelinessto depression, panic,
> hypersensitivity, diminished self-worth, and a loss
> of perspective.

In essence, culture shock is the loss of internal balance—the feeling of disorientation, confusion, uncertainty, and apprehension that we experience when we move from a familiar environment, where we have learned to perform and conduct our daily routines effortlessly and productively, to an environment that we are unfamiliar with, where we are unable to function at our usual level.

Travelers are often disoriented, anxious, depressed, or hostile, and become dissatisfied with their new life. What tends to aggravate the situation is a nagging feeling that this state will never go away.

Sufferers from culture shock often do not recognize what is happening. They just know that something is wrong, and feel miserable. They often deny the possibility that culture shock might be the problem, and shift their focus to others, attributing their distress to the people around them.

> ### WHY DOES CULTURE SHOCK OCCUR?
> Psychologists agree that the basic cause of culture shock
> is "change overload," resulting from the sudden loss
> of everything that is familiar.

Change overload is caused by two factors. The first is the move itself, handling the scores of changes that occur, including coping with the loss of the comforts and familiarity of the previous lifestyle, adjusting to the new and strange environment, and reestablishing all the details of everyday life.

The second factor is intercultural contact—the all-embracing and relentless contact with the unfamiliar culture. Culture shock occurs as a result of the persistent and draining effort involved in making sense of the new environment and its cultural rules, attempting to function within its boundaries, and adapting to it.

The more intensive the contact with the new environment, and the more changes the newcomer has to accommodate, the more taxing this phase is likely to be.

As noted earlier, the culture-shock experience is part of a much larger and more significant process that is essential for successful relocation—the cross-cultural adaptation process (reviewed in Chapter 8). In fact, it is the cross-cultural learning and adaptation process, along with the psychological challenges it presents, that induces culture shock.

WHO MIGHT EXPERIENCE CULTURE SHOCK?
Anyone and everyone who moves abroad is vulnerable to culture shock. The predictable symptoms may surface regardless of nationality, country of origin, or country of destination.

Culture shock can affect all who move abroad. This includes settlers, who relocate with the intention to live permanently in the new country, as well as sojourners, who are staying only temporarily. Inexperienced travelers and tourists are also vulnerable.

In a typical year, millions of people leave the safety of their own countries and the comforts of their homes, and plunge, temporarily at least, into foreign cultures. Not all experience culture shock, but the vast majority do.

Culture shock is not confined to adults. Children and teenagers, too, often experience it.

> ### WHEN IS CULTURE SHOCK LIKELY TO OCCUR?
> Moving to an unfamiliar country can immediately
> bring on culture shock. More common, however,
> is the delayed culture shock that tends to appear
> after the settling-in period.
> Culture shock may also occur on repatriation after
> a lengthy period spent abroad. This is known as
> "reverse culture shock."

Some travelers experience the symptoms of culture shock early in their journey, and this can be triggered by exposure to unfamiliar living conditions that may be considered intolerable, arduous, or substandard by the visitor. For example, a tourist from a Western country who travels to a developing country might immediately be upset or saddened by the living conditions that seem common and acceptable to the locals, such as poverty, deprivation, lack of food or water, or poor medical facilities. Thus, he or she is likely to feel the symptoms of culture shock early on in their journey.

However, delayed culture shock is much more common, and often occurs after the settling-in period. It is when the honeymoon comes to an end that the visitor begins to realize the endless minute details that must be addressed. Cultural differences in behavior and values also become more noticeable at this point, and the visitor begins to grasp the massive learning curve that lies ahead. This is when he or she moves into the shock phase.

Reverse culture shock is often experienced on reentry to the homeland. While culture shock is a widely recognized phenomenon, reverse culture shock is less well known. Many people believe the process of repatriation will be straightforward, because they are returning home to a place they know well and where they feel comfortable. They don't expect to face the types of challenges they experienced when they moved abroad. As a result, many are taken by surprise.

> ### *HOW LONG DOES CULTURE SHOCK LAST?*
> Culture shock can last for minutes, hours, weeks, or months, and, in some severe cases, years. There is also evidence to suggest that most people who relocate experience several repetitive episodes of culture shock.

There are several factors that affect both the duration and the severity of the experience. The first is the length of stay. As might be expected, short-term visitors such as tourists and businesspeople tend to experience mild and brief episodes of culture shock, which can be felt for minutes or hours. Most are likely to ignore it, and then probably forget about it by the time they return home.

Expatriates, diplomats, overseas students, and others who relocate temporarily, yet for an extended period of time, tend to experience a relatively short span of culture shock, which can last from days to weeks, or, in more severe cases, for months.

Immigrants often report a lengthy and more intense culture-shock experience, which can last for weeks or months, and, in some cases, for years. These episodes of culture shock tend to occur in repetitive cycles.

The differences between these groups can be explained by "temporariness psychology." Knowing that a particular situation is temporary helps us to treat any obstacle or difficulty in a more relaxed manner and with more resilience than if we think, or know, that it is permanent. Also, the knowledge that we have a place to go back to where we are comfortable and in control renders us more confident and resilient.

Importantly, there is evidence today to suggest that the culture-shock experience is not limited to international relocation. It can occur when we move to a new school, a new job, or a different city. This is because we have to adapt to a new subculture (such as an organizational, class, ethnic, racial, professional, or local culture) within our own country. Obviously, the culture shock experienced during international relocation differs from other transitions in its scale and intensity.

The degree of resemblance or difference between the homeland culture and the host culture also affects the extent to which culture shock is felt, in terms of both time span and intensity. Of course, the more similarities we find between the host and the homeland cultures, the more moderate the culture-shock experience is likely to be.

Another factor that affects the intensity and scale of culture shock is prior knowledge and familiarity with the destination country and its culture. This is significantly influenced by the type and extent of the preparation and training travelers have had before their arrival.

Previous relocation experience and personality traits also make some people more immune to culture shock than others. These traits include positivity, resilience, flexibility, adaptability, self-awareness, curiosity, willingness to learn, and a sense of humor.

The availability of a support system in the destination country is also a significant factor that can shorten and lessen the effects of culture shock. Diplomats and expatriates are examples of visitors who often enjoy a strong support system, which includes their colleagues at work, most of whom are likely to be their fellow countrymen.

PHASES OF CULTURE SHOCK
Studies that have analyzed the course of the culture-shock experience have identified several phases:
+ Disorientation (or transition shock, reviewed in Chapter 16)
+ Disillusionment
+ Rejection
+ Regression
+ Distress
+ Recovery and Acceptance

These phases of culture shock are not always linear. Some people skip some of them, or experience them at the same time. However, they are cumulative in nature: they tend to build up, with symptoms escalating from one phase to another, creating an emotional snowball effect that culminates in the distress phase. Understanding the progression of culture shock is of particular importance for any intervention aimed at preventing, circumventing, or easing the symptoms.

WHAT ARE THE LONG-TERM EFFECTS OF CULTURE SHOCK?

Culture shock is often portrayed as an upsetting and disruptive experience, and yet the majority of visitors recover with no long-term effects.

Though it may be a painful and disruptive experience, most people recover from culture shock without any need for medical or psychological intervention. Indeed, many people experience culture shock as a mild, transitory annoyance that can be overcome with relative ease through conscious effort and increased knowledge.

However, this is not always the case, and a minority of travelers do experience long-term effects. In my work, I have come across people who are unhappy and uncomfortable in their host country, never really settling in. For these people, culture shock has led to incomplete psychological or social integration in the host culture, resulting in underperformance and social marginalization. For others, the time it takes to adapt and function at their normal standards claims a heavy price. For the few, the psychological symptoms of culture shock, manifested in depression, anxiety, and lack of confidence, are continuous, and they never make a full or reasonable recovery. And, as we have seen, in some cases the inability to cope with culture shock can lead to interruption of the relocation assignment and premature return.

These negative, long-term outcomes often occur because travelers are unwilling to learn, and consequently, unable to adapt.

PREVENTION, MODERATION, COPING, AND RECOVERY

Can culture shock be prevented or moderated? Are there any tools that can help newcomers cope and recover quickly? The answer is "Yes!" Though not all aspects of culture shock can be avoided, the discomforts can be significantly lessened and their duration shortened to enable a quick recovery.
This is what this part of the book is about!

Culture shock is a period of intense cultural learning, self-assessment, and growth. It signals that you are learning about and adapting to the local culture, and, presumably, this is what you want to do!

I believe everyone can learn to manage international transitions successfully and cope effectively with culture shock.

The following chapters guide you through this taxing experience. The goal here is to prepare you for your journey, so that you will be able to foresee, prevent, or clear some of the hurdles your move may present. You will also discover effective ways to manage your psychological state so that you will be able to moderate or ease the culture-shock symptoms, and recover quickly.

Moving beyond culture shock puts you on the path to becoming interculturally fluent. Becoming more deeply engaged with the local culture increases your level of adaptation, and your ability to accomplish your relocation goals with success.

Undoubtedly, knowledge and preparation matter, and can make the difference between success and failure.

Chapter 18

STAGES AND SYMPTOMS OF CULTURE SHOCK

The purpose of this chapter is to provide you with essential knowledge on the causes, symptoms, and phases of the culture-shock experience. This information will enable you to recognize whether you or others around you are going through culture shock, and to take the necessary action to address and moderate the symptoms.

In what follows, each stage of the culture-shock experience is described in detail, highlighting the typical symptoms.

THE DISILLUSIONMENT PHASE

At this point in the relocation journey newcomers have probably progressed significantly with their initial arrangements. They may have settled into their new home, got a car, registered their children to school, and perhaps started working or studying. They are now beginning to establish their new everyday routines.

The enthusiasm and euphoria of the honeymoon phase have now faded, and a sense of disillusionment takes over as newcomers have to face the realities of day-to-day living, and are required to address some challenges and obstacles that their new routines may present to them.

The disorientation and confusion of the previous phase now turns into self-doubt and loss of confidence. They recognize the huge learning curve that awaits them, and as a result, they may question the wisdom of their relocation.

They may ask themselves, "What have I gotten myself into? What am I doing here? Will I be able to cope with this? Will I ever be able to feel comfortable here? Will I find new friends? What do I do if I can't cope?"

Language learning and communication may not be as easy as they expected, and they may be unable to convey their thoughts and feelings. The inability to communicate often becomes a significant source of frustration at this point. As a result of their inability to communicate, local people may treat them as children, which can make them feel incompetent, unintelligent, helpless, and vulnerable—in fact, "like a child."

During this phase, travelers are likely to become aware that some of their actions or manners—even those that were rewarded and valued at home—are ineffective when interacting with locals, and that their habitual behavior receives a negative response—it is perhaps ignored, ridiculed, or seen as offensive. This awareness is often followed by a drop in self-confidence, with excessive introspection and self-monitoring.

In order to adapt well and integrate, our sense of self has to be expanded and modified, and this puts our identity and sense of authenticity at risk. We become aware that there are different ways of living, working, and establishing relationships, and our deep-rooted notions about how to behave and how to do things are threatened. We have to integrate our new experiences and reactions into our "old self," and, as a result, our self-identity is shaken.

Our family and friends—the people we would normally turn to at times of need—are now far away and may not understand what we are going through. A psychological gap begins to develop. As a result, we may feel even more lonely and isolated.

During this stage, newcomers may not be able to identify what is upsetting them. They are aware, however, of the growing feeling of self-doubt, loss of confidence, and stress, and may be disproportionately upset by small things. It is this state of agitation and hypersensitivity that leads to the next phase.

"Mom, What if I Need to Go to the Toilet?"
I'd like to share with you my first culture-shock slump.

It was my daughter's third day at school. She was four years old. On the first two days I was able to sit with her in the classroom, but today I had been asked to sit outside.

As we went into the school, my daughter, clutching my hand, now looked scared and lost. She whispered, "Mom, what do I do if I need to go to the toilet?"

I frantically racked my brains for the right words, and immediately realized that I didn't know what she should say. My little girl now had tears in her eyes, and my heart sank. I felt useless, helpless, and irresponsible. Somehow, I pulled myself together to promise her that I would ask the teacher before the lesson began.

As I left the classroom it dawned on me that if I couldn't help my child with this simplest thing, how on earth would I manage to do a Ph.D. here? I sat down in the empty corridor, feeling depressed and anxious, and wept.

THE REJECTION PHASE
At this phase in the relocation journey, cultural differences in behavior and values become more obvious. Newcomers may now begin to see the deeper differences between the new environment and their homeland. What previously seemed new and exciting is now incomprehensible, strange, and frustrating.

Members of the host society are by this time expecting them to behave as they do. On occasion, the way that the newcomer was accustomed to behaving before is considered odd or unacceptable in the new place.

Newcomers now recognize the weight and significance of having to make a complete cultural adjustment. It is not as easy as anticipated. The loss of social cues is also acutely recognized now and, as a result, they may feel alienated, separated from others, and lonely.

The core of this phase of culture shock concerns our values and beliefs. We have been brought up to believe in certain things, and when we relocate, the differences that we notice in lifestyle, values, and beliefs may make us challenge our own. The inability to make use of our own cultural resources, which are very much a part of our identity, accentuates the sense of alienation and frustration.

Many newcomers report a feeling of being a stranger, unwelcome, and redundant. The strongest feeling is, "I don't belong; I don't fit in."

In moving abroad and changing cultures, they inevitably changed their own status. Back home they were somebody. Their place in society was known and established. Here, in these new surroundings, they are nobody. As foreigners they are members of minority groups who may be marginalized and even stigmatized, and whose voices count for little or nothing.

They may also find that their homeland, so dear to them, is looked upon negatively, regarded with suspicion, or dismissed as insignificant.

They may struggle with perceptions or assumptions about them, based on their nationality, ethnicity, race, gender, dress, or even hairstyle. In a nutshell, they find themselves in circumstances that diminish their self-worth.

In reaction to this feeling of alienation, many newcomers start to perceive everything around them in a negative light. They disapprove of or complain about the new environment and regard it as inferior to their homeland, and might become antagonistic to everything about the host country.

> The clearest signs of the rejection phase are hostility, criticism, and rejection of the host culture.

As troubles and challenges mount up, they are likely to look around for help, which may not be easily forthcoming. They may conclude that the locals are either unable to comprehend their difficulties, or are indifferent to them, and dismiss them all as selfish and insensitive. This triggers the hostility to the new environment that is one of the surest signs of culture shock.

Another sign of this phase is an "us and them" attitude, accompanied by typical "blame them" indicators: "These people are so cold and unfriendly!" "Things here are so confusing and inefficient!"

An additional stumbling block that compounds the problem is a tendency to think of members of other cultures in terms of stereotypes: the excitable Arabs; the amorous French; the lazy Latinos; the materialistic Americans. It has been noted that anxiety-prone people tend to cling to stereotypes, because it helps them to lower the threat of the unknown by making the world seem more predictable. What victims of culture shock desperately need is a familiar, predictable world. The trouble with such labels is that they obstruct any sensible, realistic, or fair-minded assessment of the host society and its customs, and therefore delay the recovery from the state of culture shock.

Inevitably, the newcomer's hostile reaction increases the gap between the unhappy visitor and those around him, because people sense his antagonism and begin to avoid him and minimize their interaction with him. The outcome is social isolation.

A very common complaint voiced by newcomers is loneliness and homesickness: missing friends, places, favorite leisure activities, foods, TV shows. They are tired of being with unfamiliar people and having to be conscious and alert all the time. They often feel misunderstood, and the homesickness comes from the need just to be in a familiar environment, where they can be immediately understood, and comfortable with people around them. This phase can generate mental and physical fatigue, emotional drain, and stress.

A mature, confident person may be able to shrug off these circumstances and events; but if the newcomer is insecure, sensitive, or shy, they can seem overwhelming to him.

This longing and constant comparison between "life here" and "life back home" marks the beginning of the next phase: regression.

THE REGRESSION PHASE

In this phase of culture shock, the cultural differences become a source of discord and conflict. Friction can occur between people of different cultures when those involved have no knowledge of the other's cultural background. When this happens, newcomers are likely to reject and avoid contact with local people, and view them as the cause of their discomfort.

Newcomers in this phase tend to withdraw from contact with members of the host society and seek refuge among their own countrymen or people who speak their language and who they feel will understand what they are going through. Much of the time together is spent watching films, reading newspapers, surfing Web sites, and consuming books, music, food, and anything else they can get from home. Another favorite pastime is complaining about the host country and its culture, and comparing things "here" to those "back home." They find relief in passing judgment and grumbling about features of the host society.

These discussions almost never lead to an honest evaluation of the situation, or the awareness that the difficulty may lie in the attitude of the critics themselves. They are simply gripe sessions, in which the virtues of the home country are exaggerated almost as much as the alleged failings of the host country. As Oberg notes, "When foreigners get together to grouse about the host country and its people, you can be sure they are suffering from culture shock."

> The more we perceive the differences between the cultures in a judgmental way, the more severe the culture shock is likely to be.

The frequent comparisons between "home" and "here" make life in the homeland seem so much better. The difficulties and problems there are forgotten, and only the good things are remembered. The homeland suddenly seems very attractive, and newcomers may find themselves wondering why they ever left, or wishing to be back where things are "normal," "right," and "make sense." They may question the sanity or normality of the locals, as well as how "proper," "right," or "good" things are.

Underlying much of the confusion that newcomers experience is the fact that even if they speak the language of the country, there are endless opportunities for misunderstanding. Experts in cross-cultural communication argue that language is just a small part of our communication, and that it is supported by hundreds of vocal nuances, as well as facial expressions, body language, and gestures that can easily be misread. Consequently, language learning may stall, or even go into reverse, with visitors deciding that their own language is acceptable for most situations.

The best way to illustrate this phase of culture shock is to give an example. Here is an extract from a blog by a young woman who relocated from the UK to Israel, describing her own culture-shock experience.

On Cultural Differences and Buying Swimsuits
Katrina Jacobs

After a few months, I left the familiarity of Jerusalem to find work in Tel Aviv. Having grown up in the UK, I was excited by the prospect of living near a sunny beach and decided to buy a bikini to celebrate. I entered a shop where the sales assistant, busy talking on her mobile phone and writing in a book, acknowledged my presence by nodding and waving her hand in the direction of the costumes.

I picked out a bikini and went behind the curtain in the corner to try it on. While I was in the middle of changing, the assistant put her head round the curtain, offering help and insisting that I come out of the cubicle to look in the mirror. I felt somewhat uncomfortable exposing my bikini-clad body in the middle of the shop, but ventured out, as there appeared to be no choice.

Looking at my reflection, I heard the assistant make a loud tutting sound. Then, without warning, she grabbed the swimsuit bottom, lifting it higher on my leg, and put her hand down my bikini top to adjust its position. Shaking her head, she then pointed to my thighs and said, in a genuinely sympathetic tone, "I'm fat there, too!"

Astounded by the assistant's "helpfulness," I hurriedly dressed and rushed out of the shop, politely declining the offer of more flattering costumes.

Rude or honest, intrusive or helpful, humiliating or entertaining—what would be your assessment of this shopping experience?

Having previously bought swimwear only in the comfort of Marks and Spencer's, I was personally horrified. I left the shop asking myself if it was practical to live in Israel, yet do all my clothes shopping on visits to the UK, or should I never wear a swimming costume again for fear of offending passers-by with my thighs?

Had I had more experience in Israel, I might have understood that the assistant's directness was much more to do with culture than it was to do with clothes size. In fact, many elements of this story reflect cultural orientations. The unannounced entrance into the cubicle and the bikini adjustment are classic examples of the Israeli concept of personal space (or lack of it), whereas I saw it as intrusive, bordering on physical molestation. Even the assistant's reception, nodding to me while talking on her phone and writing, illustrates the strong tendency of Israelis to multitask, and may not have just been bad customer service, as I initially judged.

Two years after moving to Israel, when even simple activities such as going to the bank or supermarket still presented a formidable challenge to my patience and sanity, I began seriously to question my relocation. Later I learned that many of my negative perceptions of Israelis were not wholly accurate, and I was, in fact, suffering from a severe case of culture shock.

Furthermore, I learned that, with information and practical strategies, much can be done to minimize culture shock.*

THE DISTRESS PHASE

This is the phase in which everything combines to bring the newcomer to a state of depression.

The contribuing factors include the strain caused by change overload and the constant effort to adapt; the sense of loss and feelings of deprivation in relation to friends, status, profession, and possessions; feelings of rejection by or

*Source: http://www.hagshama.org.il/en

rejecting members of the new culture; the confusion in roles, values, and self-identity; and the frustration, anxiety, or disgust about "foreign practices." The feeling of helplessness, inability to solve simple problems, and the lack of confidence in our ability to cope with the new environment are now deeply felt. All these mount up, creating an emotional snowball effect that culminates in the distress phase.

Newcomers may experience moodiness, hypersensitivity, and a mixed bag of other feelings, such as stress, anger, confusion, hostility, indecision, frustration, fear, sadness, loneliness, homesickness, being excluded or overlooked, estrangement or feeling abused, helplessness, incompetence, and inability to take charge of their lives.

Minor frustrations, delays, or inconveniences are responded to with irritation, anger, or resentment and loss of self control that is out of proportion to the cause. Some people are disproportionately fearful or suspicious, thinking that the locals are out to cheat them. Another symptom can be over-concern about the cleanliness or hygiene of drinking water, food, or dishes.

Those who experience this phase tend to become nervous and unusually tired. They may experience unexplainable crying, allergies, headaches, upset stomach, insomnia, desire to sleep too much or too little, overeating or loss of appetite, skin complaints, and, at times, sexual problems.

Travelers who reach this phase view their new world with resentment and frustration, and alternate between being angry at others for not understanding them, and being filled with self-pity, and a deep sense of inadequacy and vulnerability. They are likely to have serious doubts about their decision to relocate. However, due to their psychological state, they may not be able to make any decisions.

In terms of severity, the depressive state rarely becomes clinical. It tends to appear in short outbreaks of depression or moodiness. These can last a minute, an hour, a day, or even a few weeks, but are relatively short and often arrive in repetitive cycles, known clinically as "stress–recovery–adaptation–growth" cycles.

Culture shock is a psychological illness, and, as is true of other mental conditions, the victims usually do not know that they are afflicted. Newcomers are often unaware of the degree to which they are exhibiting these symptoms. They may recognize that they are miserable and that the advice offered to them—such as, "be patient"; "work hard"; "learn the language"—does not seem to help.

The distress phase can be avoided, and its symptoms lessened, by taking appropriate action both in the phases leading up to it and when it occurs. There are many ways to address this situation and relieve the depression (see Chapter 19). The most effective way, however, is to be prepared for it, so that it does not come as a surprise.

All these feelings may make it difficult to deal with residents of the host country. Many newcomers attempt to solve the problem by withdrawing into themselves. They refuse to learn the native language, make no effort to find friends among the local people, and take no interest in local history, art, architecture, or any other aspect of the host culture.

Some newcomers develop a noticeable over-dependence on people from their own country who experienced culture shock themselves, but who are now living successfully and happily in the host country. If those veterans can draw on their experience and wisdom, and react with sympathy, patience, and understanding toward the newcomers, they may be able to alleviate their distress. Furthermore, the mere fact that they have been through it, have survived, and are now leading successful and comfortable lives, has an exemplary effect.

Be kind to yourself, and give yourself time to adjust. However, if you are finding it extremely difficult to cope, or are experiencing severe symptoms, do seek counseling immediately. (See exercise in Chapter 19.)

Culture shock is undeniably a disconcerting experience. Nevertheless, it has an array of advantages. It can be seen as a transitional experience, important for personal growth in a new environment. It is also a mind-stretching process that will leave you with broader perspectives, deeper insight into yourself, and greater tolerance of other people.

Once it is harnessed, it can produce many beneficial results. These may include increased intellectual, emotional, and behavioral fitness, the ability to communicate competently in the host environment, increased psychological balance, and the development of intercultural identity.

> Culture shock is to be expected. It is a normal part of the adjustment process, and, with time, the symptoms will dissipate as the newcomer integrates into the new culture.

Remember, everyone is different. Therefore, the symptoms and stages of culture shock described here are in no way complete or universal. As we have seen , the duration and extent to which one is immersed in a new environment influences the degree to which culture shock occurs. As a result, while the U-curve description in Chapter 8 may be accurate for many, there are people who won't experience any type of culture shock or who will experience the stages in entirely different sequences. Nevertheless, by expecting some bumps in the road, and by being aware of potential difficulties and possible reasons for them, you will find that the challenges associated with going abroad can be more easily managed.

THE RECOVERY AND ACCEPTANCE PHASE

This phase marks the beginning of the upward slope of adaptation, in which acceptance and gradual recovery take place. It tends to last between several weeks and several months.

At this stage some of the exaggerated expectations that newcomers bring with them are tempered, and become more realistic. They can find the energy and motivation to address the new challenges and to take charge of the learning and adaptation process.

Central aspects of the new environment have now been mastered. Newcomers begin to establish a small comfort zone, within which they feel secure and in control. They can now cope successfully with everyday routines and experience satisfaction on overcoming the initial relocation challenges.

At this point, they are becoming more familiar and comfortable with the host culture. They are beginning to understand, accept, and enjoy some aspects of it, and can respond correctly to cultural and social cues. They may experience a sense of relief as they start to relax in their new environment, and their perception of their own lives is more balanced. Increased command of the language also occurs at this point, which can help to generate the upward slant.

Newcomers have come to terms with the changes that have taken place in their lives and have come to accept them. They are likely to evaluate the positives and negatives of the host country against those back home in a more objective way, and realize that the problems and negative aspects of the new country are not reserved for foreigners—even the natives find certain things difficult. With this acceptance comes the realization that the new country is not better or worse than others—it's just different.

As familiarity with local language and customs increases, the newcomers' self-confidence and self-esteem begin to return. They are likely to feel safer and less negative toward the local people, and as soon as they become friendlier the locals, too, seem less hostile. Slowly, they progress from a grudging acceptance of their surroundings to a genuine fondness for them, and they can be proud of their growing ability to function in the new society. Often new networks and friendships are formed, which can relieve some of the distress felt earlier.

Importantly, their sense of humor will have returned, and they may find that they are able to look at themselves and laugh. They may well wonder what made them so unhappy before. At last they feel comfortable and at ease in the new place. It's not so bad!

REVERSE CULTURE SHOCK

While the notion of culture shock may be familiar, the idea of reverse culture shock is much less so.

"Return" or "reverse" culture shock occurs on repatriation—when expatriates, diplomats, volunteers, overseas students, emigrants, or other travelers return to their homeland.

Most people think that because they are going "home," where everything is familiar, the process of acclimatization should be quite easy. They don't expect to have to adjust, as they did when they first relocated abroad. However, it is precisely because of this expectation that reverse culture shock is triggered, and this is also why it often feels daunting and overwhelming.

While you lived abroad, images of "home" may have become idealized or romanticized. It is easy to forget, or play down, the issues that were once a source of stress in your everyday life. Reencountering them can be disconcerting.

You have been away for a long time, becoming comfortable with the habits and customs of a different culture. You have probably matured and changed considerably. The people around you generally expect you to be the person you were when you left, and are likely to treat you in the same way as they did before.

Also, just as you have changed, you are returning to a group of people and a country that will have changed. These changes will affect the way you are accepted by your own country and people, as well as how you perceive and accept them.

Most people at home are likely to be unfamiliar with the concept of reverse culture shock, and may often respond to a returnee having difficulty readjusting by bluntly suggesting they "get over it."

Following the stimulation of your time abroad, a return to family, friends, and old routines, however nice and comforting, can seem dull. It is natural to miss the excitement and discovery that characterized your life in a foreign country, and sharing your stories may be a way of recreating this for yourself—but do remember that others may not find your stories as exciting as you do.

Just as the initial culture shock has definable stages and a relatively predictable progression, so does the reverse shock. The honeymoon phase of initial euphoria, or at least relief to be home, is often present for some time, followed by some degree of irritation and alienation, with an eventual readjustment. The "U-shaped" adjustment curve on page 105 that illustrates the adjustment to life overseas can be modified to a "W," showing the reentry process.

While the phases are similar, their duration may differ. Both the honeymoon and the culture-shock phases are likely to be much shorter upon reentry.

Although there are many of reasons for looking forward to going home, reentry can at times be as challenging and as frustrating as adjusting to life overseas. Indeed, it may take a while to become at ease with the cues, signs, and symbols of your home culture.

Contrary to the expectation that going "home" is a simple matter of resuming your earlier routines and reestablishing prior relationships, reentry has its own set of special social and psychological adjustments.

There are, of course, many ways to prevent and address the reverse culture-shock experience, and these are similar to the ones you found useful when moving abroad.

Chapter 19

MANAGING CULTURE SHOCK

The earlier chapters described the symptoms and phases of culture shock. Here the focus is on how to cope with culture shock, if and when it occurs.

As we have seen, one of the baffling things about culture shock is that its symptoms are varied and can be easily misunderstood or overlooked. Furthermore, the term "shock" is not always appropriate. Culture shock is deceptively gradual. Symptoms are often very mild at first, and can progress toward depression rather slowly.

The severity or intensity of culture shock can be described in terms of five levels (see below). Note that some people never reach the "shock" level, and simply experience mild irritation and temporary discontent. However, some people pass quickly though these levels, and experience culture shock as a profoundly disorienting and demoralizing experience, from which they may take much longer to recover.

Culture Shock Has Five Levels of Severity
+ **Cultural surprise.** This usually occurs early on in the relocation journey, when travelers are beginning to explore the unfamiliar culture.
+ **Cultural tension.** This is mild annoyance and tension that builds up as a result of the constant effort to function in an uncomfortable setting.
+ **Cultural frustration.** This is a repetitive state in which newcomers react strongly to cultural behavior that they find upsetting.

✦ **Cultural fatigue.** This is one of the common symptoms of "change overload." It occurs when travelers attempt to take in, adapt to, and react to too much at once. The result is psychological exhaustion.

✦ **Cultural shock.** This is a result of cultural clashes— misunderstandings or friction that arise in cross-cultural situations. The shock comes from the draining psychological effort to accommodate to the demands of the new environment while maintaining some form of cultural authenticity.

The aim of the following notes and action points is to help you contain the culture shock, and to keep it at the lower levels of intensity.

COPING STRATEGIES FOR WHEN CULTURE SHOCK STRIKES
Be Prepared!

✦ First and foremost, know that it is coming, and be prepared for it. Part of the shock is not expecting it. Now that you have read this book, you know there is nothing strange or abnormal about it.

✦ Be aware of the symptoms. If you think you are experiencing culture shock, read Chapter 18, and do the self-assessment exercise below.

✦ Once you have verified that you are experiencing culture shock, you can take steps to deal with it.

Keep a Relocation Journal

One of the best ways to follow your own state, and at the same time to record your time abroad, is to write a journal or a blog.

✦ A journal allows you to have an internal dialog with yourself, and also to look back upon your experiences and see the ups and downs as they occurred.

✦ Your journal can be an invaluable account of your travels, which you may only appreciate in retrospect.

✦ It can be therapeutic to express yourself openly in ways you might not want to do even to a close friend.

✦ People who do this regularly can look back and detect patterns that were not clear when they occurred.

✦ This kind of record might reveal important issues that are causing you stress, and make you more conscious of these.

✦ Importantly, this type of log will enable you to take action early before symptoms or problems intensify.

The following exercise is designed to help you assess whether you, or anyone around you, is suffering from culture shock.

✍️ CULTURE-SHOCK SELF-ASSESSMENT EXERCISE

1. First, read Chapter 18, about the symptoms of culture shock, and identify the phase you are in.
2. What symptoms are you experiencing or have you experienced in the past week? Check the relevant boxes.

Physical symptoms
- ❑ Headaches
- ❑ Upset stomach, overeating, or loss of appetite
- ❑ Allergies: breathing or skin problems
- ❑ Fatigue, insomnia, or desire to sleep too much
- ❑ Unexplained crying
- ❑ Hypochondria
- ❑ Excessive drinking or recreational drug dependency
- ❑ Sexual problems

Psychological symptoms
Indicative symptoms:
- ❑ Excessive criticism of the host culture
- ❑ Confusion or feeling disoriented
- ❑ Extreme loneliness or homesickness
- ❑ Hostility or resentment toward local people
- ❑ Feelings of not belonging or fitting in, alienation, or estrangement
- ❑ Feeling that you are being excluded or overlooked

Other symptoms:
- ❑ Moodiness
- ❑ Loss of focus or inability to complete tasks
- ❑ Indecision
- ❑ Frustration
- ❑ Stress
- ❑ Anger
- ❑ Fear
- ❑ Suspicion of others, extreme concern about safety
- ❑ Over-concern about hygiene
- ❑ Extreme concerns over being taken advantage of

❑ Feeling depressed or sad
❑ Inability to take charge of your life
❑ Impatience
❑ Lack of self-control
❑ Overreacting or exaggerating
❑ Easily irritated or aggravated by small things, hypersensitivity
❑ Feeling vulnerable, helpless, or incompetent

Now, look at your symptoms. Note how many indicative symptoms you have, if any. (If you have none, then it is likely that you are not experiencing culture shock.) The number and type of symptoms you have will give you an indication of how severe your culture shock is.

Assuming you have recognized the symptoms of culture shock in yourself or others, the next step is to take action and alleviate some of the symptoms.

Restore a Sense of Normality
✦ Remember that what you are experiencing is perfectly normal, and that you are not alone in this.
✦ Know that the symptoms are temporary, and that they will go away soon.
✦ Build on your past experience. After all, this is not the first time you have adjusted to a new environment.
✦ Relax! The problem isn't you. You are new and need to learn a lot, and being a newcomer is a perfectly legitimate place to be.
✦ Pay attention to your health: make sure you exercise, eat well, and rest enough.
✦ If you feel that you don't fit in, remind yourself that you are new, and that it is legitimate for someone who is new to be different!

Manage Your Expectations

✦ Our expectations affect how we interpret events and what we feel about others and ourselves. Adopt realistic expectations that empower you.

✦ Be realistic in your expectations of yourself. Learning a new language, adapting to a new culture, and learning the details of your new life will take time. Give yourself that time!

✦ Realize that often a negative experience is not personal but cultural.

✦ When things are not going well, stop and try to figure out why.

✦ Don't be too hard on yourself when you are not perfect, or when things don't go as expected.

> Culture shock is 10 percent what happens to us, and 90 percent how we interpret it or react to it!

Maintain a Positive Attitude

✦ Set small goals for yourself (for example, to learn two new foreign phrases each day), and stick to them.

✦ Focus on solutions, not on problems. Separate the issues that cause you distress, and deal with one issue at a time.

✦ Encourage family members to acknowledge their feelings and support each other.

✦ Look back to see what you have achieved. Learn from your experiences.

✦ Always look for the best, not the worst, in your situation. People who go around looking for trouble usually find it.

Establish a Contentment Zone

✦ Stick to the positive routines or habits that help you to relax and unwind, and that generally make you feel good.

managing culture shock

✦ Look after yourself. Do something you enjoy on a daily basis, and arrange something pleasant to look forward to.

✦ Make sure you have a few comfort items and familiar things around you.

✦ Go out and interact with people. Don't sit around being negative and critical; this just prolongs and deepens your gloom.

✦ Maintain a balance: keep busy and see other people, but beware of becoming over-stimulated and exhausted. Take time to be on your own, relax, and reflect.

Engage With Your Cultural Learning Process

✦ Allow yourself to explore the new culture, take time to learn it, and understand the differences between the cultures.

✦ Don't be afraid to do things you haven't done before. Try new foods, explore the local arts and music, visit new places.

✦ Keep using the language, even if you find it difficult.

✦ Be curious! The best way to lower your criticism and avoid the slump in your morale is to maintain your curiosity about the new culture and people.

✦ Learn new ways of doing things.

✦ Be flexible and adaptable, without abandoning your core values or compromising your sense of self.

✦ Find ways to make your adaptation process as efficient and as pleasant as possible (see Chapter 16).

✦ Don't become judgmental about the country and the people. This often triggers the next phases of culture shock.

> Don't be afraid to fail!
> Nothing risked is nothing gained,
> especially while abroad.

Develop and Maintain Social Support

+ Go out, see people. Socialize with people you know well and are comfortable with on a regular basis, to relieve feelings of loneliness. Share your feelings with others, and seek their advice and experience.
+ Discuss with others the disadvantages you have discovered and are critical about, and find ways to work around them.
+ Stay in touch with people back home.

Returning Home Prematurely

Despite all your efforts, there may be times when you feel you are getting nowhere. You may be stressed, tired, fed up, and wondering why you decided to put yourself through all this. You may feel a strong urge to get on the first flight back home.

Do not return to your homeland while you are experiencing episodes of culture shock! Be aware that you are not in the best shape to make decisions at this point.

Furthermore, if you leave now you will keep the negative experience in your mind for the rest of your life, as well as the low self-esteem, feelings of failure, and negative perceptions toward your host country.

I therefore strongly recommend you to wait until you recover, and only then to make a sound and more informed decision.

Seeking Help

As noted above, for a minority of newcomers the shock of transition and adapting to a new country and a new life can be too much to handle. Grappling with the losses incurred and dealing with unfamiliar and often challenging situations can trigger serious depression that may require treatment.

Teenagers, in particular, are vulnerable in these situations. Therefore, it is important to be conscious of their emotional state and provide support and professional help when needed.

Thus, if the measures suggested here don't work for you, or for someone around you, seek help in the form of medical advice or counseling.

The following is a culture-shock management exercise that is designed to help you manage the symptoms.

✍ CULTURE-SHOCK MANAGEMENT EXERCISE

This exercise is designed to help you cope with culture shock when it occurs. Simply answer the following questions.

1. Think about your past and remind yourself of previous moves and changes that you have experienced in your life. What strengths or tools—for example, time management skills, humor, support of family, setting goals—did you use then that helped you to cope?

_____

_____

_____

_____

_____

_____

_____

_____

_____

_____

2. List below all the things that you have done successfully since your relocation journey began.

_____

_____

_____

_____

_____

_____

_____

_____

_____

_____

Give yourself a round of applause! You have done well!

3. What do you need right now to help you relax, unwind, and make you feel good? What makes you happy?

_____

_____

_____

_____

_____

_____

Now do it! Take time to do the things that make you happy.

4. List below all the things you are grateful that you have and enjoy in your life right now. This could be anything—such as your skills, resources, people who are there to support you, and many other possibilities.

_____

_____

_____

_____

_____

_____

_____

5. What is upsetting you right now? List all the problems and issues you are facing.

_____

_____

_____

_____

_____

_____

_____

6. Choose one item from this list that you wish to focus on, deal with, and bring to a close in the next days. Highlight this item.

7. The next step is planning how to handle this issue. What steps can you take to solve it? Break it down into small action steps.

The issue:

Action steps to address the issue	Due date
Step 1:	
Step 2:	
Step 3:	
Step 4:	
Step 5:	

Congratulations! You have created a plan to deal with that issue. Now act: simply take the first step! When you have completed dealing with this issue, do the same with the next.

As can be seen, when culture shock strikes there is much that you can do to relieve the symptoms and bounce back quickly.

Some people believe that experiencing culture shock is a weakness or a warning sign regarding their future success. However, the most important understanding to take away from this chapter is that culture shock is completely normal, and it is very much a part of successful adaptation. In fact, the people who experience intense culture shock are those who are most aware of themselves, and it is their self-awareness that helps them to adapt more successfully later.

Many of the tips and strategies offered here are geared toward helping you to become more conscious. You have won half the battle if you are knowledgeable, aware, and have the necessary tools to address what is coming.

The second half of the battle is putting into practice what you have learned. When culture shock strikes, keep your emotional state under control by using the unwinding and calming-down techniques offered here, and then act! Do something specific about the problems you are facing. Even taking very small steps can make a huge difference.

Chapter 20

FROM ADAPTATION TO INTEGRATION

At this stage, you have probably managed your settling-in period. You may have organized some aspects of your new life, set up new family and work routines, and established new ties. You may also have risen to challenges and cleared some hurdles along the way.

> Adaptation means initiating and accepting change in yourself in order to respond to the demands of a new environment.

Everyone adapts to a new setting to some degree, if only at the most superficial levels. Adaptation does not imply replacing your culture with a new one. It simply means adding to your existing knowledge, skills, and perspectives in order to function well in the new environment.

THE LEARNING, ADAPTATION, AND GROWTH PHASE
This phase, which can last for months and sometimes years, is signified by a sense of growth and renewed energy, which is channeled into cultural learning and behavioral adaptation. These adaptive energies encourage newcomers

to deal with cross-cultural challenges, and work to improve their functional relationship with the host society.

> In this phase, travelers develop the ability to function fully in their new environment.

By now, culture-shock regressions are largely gone, and the sense of foreignness is fading significantly. There is a general sense of contentment, comfort, and satisfaction. Most newcomers feel at ease and at home, and have a sense of belonging. They develop the ability to function fully in their new environment.

The routines and everyday practices of the host society are now understood and even appreciated. Many of the customs, habits, and differences in lifestyle that visitors struggled to accept at the beginning are now embraced as their own, practiced, and enjoyed.

Newcomers experience fewer challenges and setbacks at this point, and they can develop their own goals and aspirations.

Some people go to the extreme of rejecting their own culture. They may take on a new cultural identity, and refuse to speak their native language or associate with their own countrymen. They may view their own culture negatively, and criticize or scorn its customs and traditions.

Many expatriates, overseas students, and other temporary residents do not reach this phase, but those who do may now appreciate the privileged and exciting lifestyle they enjoy. They may embrace life overseas, no longer wanting to return to the lifestyle back home, which they see as "ordinary," or "boring."

> The adaptation process, as a learning curve, is an empowering and enriching experience, in which the newcomer expands his cultural and linguistic repertoire and develops mental and behavioral flexibility that is life-changing.

It is important to realize that many people remain stuck in the early phases of their adaptation, cutting themselves off from either their new world or the one they came from. These patterns of adaptation are unbalanced, and lead to frustration and unhappiness. Many of the difficulties and psychological complaints of foreigners in a new land, including stress and family problems, can be directly linked to incomplete adaptation.

THE INTEGRATION PHASE
The adaptation process creates the necessary foundation for social, cultural, and psychological integration.

> Integration means to become part of a society or a group, to belong to, and to participate in it.

In this phase, newcomers become integrated in all, or most, areas of life. It is the longest phase in the relocation journey, and can last for years. By now, you will have established adequate social and work ties, and your language is fluent. Communication is no longer an effort. Cultural competency is also at an adequate level. You have adopted some elements of the host culture's behavior and mentality, and may well prefer certain areas of the host culture to your own. You have acquired significant local knowledge and are involved in local life. For most people, a genuine enjoyment of the new location has developed.

Psychologically, you have settled in. In terms of your sense of belonging and identity, you no longer see yourself as a newcomer. Relocation is now a distant memory, and the host country has become "home." You have changed, and the knowledge you have acquired, and the norms and perceptions that you have adopted, have become a part of who you are. You finally learn to appreciate both your own heritage and the new way of life, and live with two cultures.

Some people gain citizenship status, and experience further changes in their social identities and sense of belonging.

Where is Home?
Our sense of place changes throughout the relocation journey.

✦ After their relocation, most visitors continue for some time to consider their homeland as their home.

✦ Many go on to experience a period of rootlessness, in which they no longer feel a sense of belonging to their homeland, but don't yet feel a sense of belonging to their host country.

✦ At a later stage, most begin to feel a sense of home in their host country, and start to perceive their homeland as a vacation resort.

✦ Some people—particularly those who visit their homeland frequently and regularly—develop a sense of belonging to both countries.

Degrees of Integration
The integration of newcomers into their host country can be described as an axis, with each person or family unit displaying different levels of social, cultural, and psychological integration. This is not an either/or state, but a continuum, and people adopt different levels and patterns of integration.

On one side of the axis is the pattern of assimilation. On the other side there is separation. In the middle, the pattern is described as integration or biculturality.

Those who assimilate are people who have adopted the norms, values, lifestyles, and identities of the host culture in a way that has led to the disappearance of their original culture. This often occurs among those who relocated at a young age.

Those who separate themselves from the host culture and people are individuals or families who live within the confines of their own immigrant, ethnic, racial, or religious group. Most expatriates seem to adopt this pattern.

Those who find the midway mark and choose to integrate tend to adopt some norms, habits, or customs of the host society and, at the same time, maintain some aspects of their heritage. They become bicultural, having learned to accommodate within themselves two cultures—two ways of thinking, two ways of making sense of the world, and two identities. As a result, they acquire behavioral flexibility, and expand their behavioral repertoire. Cultural flexibility is a powerful and very enriching capacity to have. No other experience in life can teach you that!

The exercise on the facing page is designed to help you examine your own degree of adaptation. It is meant for those who have been in their host country for at least six months, and can be repeated every few months to record progress.

✍ HAVE YOU ADJUSTED?
SELF-ASSESSMENT EXERCISE

To assess your own degree of integration, ask yourself the following questions.

1. Work / education. Do you have a job? Is this job in line with your profession? Are you upwardly or downwardly mobile or stable in your career trajectory? Is your work meaningful and satisfying?

Similar questions can be asked for education.

2. Everyday life. How well are you managing your everyday life? Do you feel comfortable and safe in your home? Are you living in temporary accommodation or a long-term place? Have you got a car? Do you have a local driver's license? Can you get around easily?

3. Your routines. Are you comfortable with your everyday routines? Is your life balanced? Do you spend enough time with your family and have enough "me" time? Have you found enjoyable things to do in your free time?

4. Finances. Have you got your finances sorted? Are you stable financially?

5. Social and work ties. Have you got social and work ties? How many, and with whom? Are your friends mainly from your homeland or local people? Do you maintain regular contact with people back home? Have you got a

support network that you can turn to for help in emergency situations and when you require assistance?

6. Local knowledge and involvement. Can you read the newspapers and follow the media? Can you find your way easily around your local area? Can you find what you require easily? What is your level of local knowledge, and how involved are you in public affairs?

7. Language. Are you making progress in the local language? Can you communicate comfortably in everyday situations?

8. Culture. Are you able to read the cultural signals of local people? Can you participate in social or cultural events and feel comfortable? Can you adapt your behavior to their expectations when you need to?

9. Identity and sense of belonging. Do you feel a sense of home here? To what extent do you feel accepted by the wider society?

10. Psychological / emotional state. Do you generally like it here? Are you satisfied with your new life? Do you have more positive than negative feelings toward the local people and their culture?

Don't be dismayed if, some time after the settling-in period, you find that you have not made as much progress as you wished in certain areas. This assessment exercise will help you to define and focus on what needs to be improved.

Cross-cultural adaptation is never perfect, and, importantly, it is never complete. However, it is also necessary to understand that being well adjusted may not mean that you truly feel a sense of belonging to your new country. Even after years abroad, you may still feel those "foreigner moments"—embarrassing cultural misunderstandings and even head-on collisions with local people over how things are done.

You may still reject and find some local norms offensive or annoying. Your language skills may never reach the fluency level, or the accent of a native-born person.

Being well adapted means that you are relaxed and adept in your new place. It means that you are comfortable in your home and your daily routine, that you can get around with reasonable confidence, and that you can function successfully in the new environment.

It means that you can understand the local language and culture and can communicate your needs to and work effectively with local people, as well as have fun and enjoy their company. It also indicates that you have built a support system around you and made some friends.

The details and fragments of your life now begin to come together and work to your satisfaction. This is when you finally feel at home.

Chapter 21

CONFRONTING A NEW CULTURE

> Moving into a new culture can feel like an exciting
> adventure, but it may, at times, feel more
> like taking part in a game
> without knowing the rules.
> The moves that other players are making don't
> make much sense, and, worse, you are
> expected to make certain
> moves but have no idea what they should be
> or when and how you should
> make them.

Culture includes thousands of minute, often vague, implied rules that derive from the values and beliefs that a group of people share, and that shape their expectations, assumptions, and attitudes. For the people who follow them, these rules are "common sense." The problem is that what is considered common sense in one culture may not make any sense in another.

No matter how open-minded you may be, there will be times when your own cultural rules will clash with those of your host country. You may find certain conventions and practices pointless, wrong, unfair, and even cruel, according to your own value system.

As you get to know the new culture and people better, you may find that some things that at first did not make sense, or even offended you, do indeed make sense in the context of their circumstances. However, some local attitudes and practices may continue to irritate or upset you, no matter how well you understand the culture.

In these cases, your self-control may be tested to the limit, but it is the only way to go about it. Making critical, condescending, or unkind remarks about the host culture is not likely to make much of a difference to the locals, but it will create a rift between you and them, probably reducing your ability to work with them effectively.

Don't assume that the local people will meet you halfway. They will expect you to adapt your behavior to theirs, and in any case may not realize that other countries have different ways of doing or perceiving things. They accept their way as the only "normal" or "proper" way.

There is no substitute for taking the time, both before and after your relocation, to make the effort to learn the cultural rules of your host country. Unfortunately, not many people do, and some pay dearly for this oversight.

Chapter 7 described in detail how to prepare for this process, and what can be learned prior to arrival to ensure a smooth entry. In this chapter, the focus is on how to handle your learning and adaptation process when it occurs in your everyday environment and when you are immersed in it, rather than in the classroom.

As we have already seen, it is the cross-cultural adaptation process that triggers culture shock. In effect, it is the relentless intercultural contact, the continuous mental effort to make sense of events, and the constant discomfort that comes from monitoring and adapting our own behavior to the new environment that drain our energy and bring about the slump in our spirits.

The adaptation process and the culture-shock experiences are interlinked in a circular manner, with one affecting the other. Thus, the better you can manage your cross-cultural adaptation process, the more effective you will be in managing and minimizing the impact of culture shock on your life. And, the more skilled you are in coping with the disturbing symptoms of culture shock, the more effective your cross-cultural learning is likely to be.

WHY ADAPTING TO A NEW CULTURE CAUSES CULTURE SHOCK

A quick look at the acculturation process detailed below reveals that it has some features that make learning and gleaning knowledge from it rather difficult.

- ✦ The process has a steep learning curve at the very beginning of the relocation journey. Most of your cultural observations, insights, and lessons are likely to occur within the first twelve months of your relocation.
- ✦ In terms of its contents and scope, cultural learning is likely to cover most, if not all, domains of life, simply because culture is embedded in every event and situation of life.
- ✦ The knowledge acquired may well be unexpected. You may find yourself taken by surprise, in even the most trivial situations, by how things are viewed or done.
- ✦ The information you acquire as you go through your acculturation process is made up of very small details of life, and is a nuanced type of knowledge that is difficult to capture, especially if you cannot communicate properly.
- ✦ The knowledge gained is often practical, and is learned by doing. Thus it directly touches your and other people's lives.
- ✦ It is a type of learning that comes from observing and engaging with the people around you. You will not have one teacher, but many informal instructors. Every person you come across can teach you something. The problem is that they may not be very competent teachers.

✦ The learning process lacks structure and is not gradual. It is often muddled and confusing You are likely to have little control over the pace or the contents of the learning. There will be times when the level of what is thrown at you will be too complicated to grasp. Sometimes the pace may be too fast, or there will be too much to take in.

✦ Because the cross-cultural adaptation learning experience is unsystematic, patchy, and fast, it is often difficult to build a coherent body of knowledge about the new culture from the events that you observe.

✦ The only group whose adaptation experience is gradual and orderly is young children. That is because they are socialized in the same way that native-born children are, and their socialization process is age-related, so that the knowledge and understanding of the society in which they are raised develops gradually.

✦ Another feature of the cross-cultural adaptation process is the unlearning process. Travelers find out quickly that some of their skills, capacities, and knowledge, as well as behavioral patterns, don't get results, or have undesired outcomes, in the new place. The process of unlearning ways of doing things and acquiring new ways is often painful. It feels like throwing away years of experience and skills, and starting from scratch. As a result of the unlearning process, many people lose their confidence, to the point that they begin to feel incompetent.

✦ In short, it is a learning process that is conducted in difficult conditions.

How then, can we handle a learning process that is patchy, disorganized, and requires unlearning? There are several strategies to help improve the quality of your cross-cultural adaptation process and enable you to glean the much needed cultural knowledge in an effective and coherent way.

MASTERING A NEW CULTURE

The cross-cultural adaptation process has two main components:

+ The first is exploration and introspection, through which you gain an understanding at a cognitive level about how to function in the new environment.
+ The second is behavioral adjustment, by which you modify and monitor your behavior in order to conform to the codes of conduct that are considered appropriate in the new place.

The way the learning and adaptation occurs is through observation, study, and reflection. At first, you learn by simply watching others and observing things as they happen, as well as by proactively asking for information and explanations, and studying the culture through more formal cultural resources, such as books, or museums. At some point, you may find yourself reflecting, making sense, and gaining understanding about how things are done in your new environment. You may compare the cultural patterns you have observed to how things are done in your homeland.

The behavioral adaptation often takes place later. It takes more time and conscious effort to emulate others and behave in similar ways, or, in some situations, to decide not to. Obviously, there are areas where you must conform in order to be able to function.

It is worth noting that in some countries there is little pressure to conform, while in others there is significant pressure to adhere to the norms.

When Holiday Songs Bring the Blues
Daria's Story

I remember my children's first Christmas celebration at school. I sat there in the audience. My six-year-old daughter was on stage with her class, dressed as an angel.

When they started singing I realized that I didn't know any of the songs, and I knew that my daughter wouldn't know them either. Her

*classmates were happily singing, but she just stood there quietly—
looking like a gloomy angel.*

*I felt so rootless, so distant from our own Jewish traditions, and so out
of place here. I resolved, for my children's sake, to keep my own heritage
alive at home, while acquainting ourselves with other religions.*

ACQUIRING CULTURAL PROFICIENCY

As you go through the phases of adjustment, your
understanding and capacity to function in the local culture
gradually increases. The process of acquiring a new culture
seems to follow the well-known competence acquisition
model that I have adapted here.

✦ Unconscious incompetence

This state is often described as "blissful ignorance." At this
point, you are likely to be unaware of cultural differences.
It may not occur to you that you may be making mistakes
or misinterpreting the behavior or communications of
those around you.

✦ Conscious incompetence

At this point, you become aware of behavioral differences.
Although you may not be able to discern or understand
what these differences are, where they occur, or how
meaningful they are, you are likely to be aware that you
are different, and realize that there are some things that
you don't understand. This realization is likely to cause
discomfort, anxiety, frustration, and loss of confidence.
This is often where the culture-shock slump occurs.

✦ Conscious competence

You now recognize that cultural differences exist, and are
able to identify what these differences are. At this phase,
you are much more aware of how your behavior is coming
across to the local people, and you may be attempting to
adapt your own behavior to accommodate the local norms.
Conscious competence means that you are making a

conscious effort to regulate your own behavior. It doesn't come naturally yet, but you are in the process of acquiring new behavior.

✦ Unconscious competence

At this point you are comfortable with your new cultural competence. You no longer have to make an effort and moderate your own behavior. Culturally appropriate behavior is now second nature to you; you can trust your instincts because they have been reconditioned by the new culture.

STRATEGIES FOR SUCCESSFUL ADAPTATION
Treat Your Adaptation as a Learning Process

The main strategy to reduce the stress involved in cross-cultural adaptation and moderate the culture-shock experience is to treat your acculturation as a learning experience, and to take charge of this process so that you can pace it in accordance with your capacities, decide what to learn, and seek the knowledge that you require.

Most people don't realize that cross-cultural adaptation is, at its core, a learning experience; that is why they become overwhelmed. But if you accept it for what it is, and take charge of the learning, this will transform your whole relocation journey.

> ### THE GIFT OF CURIOSITY
> Go out there with a real passion to learn new things, and to explore, discover, and experience a new way of life.

When you treat your relocation journey as a learning experience, you connect to resources within you, such as curiosity, open-mindedness, willingness to stretch yourself beyond your comfort zone, a capacity to tolerate uncertainty and to be in a place of not-knowing, as well as willingness to change your thinking and behavior accordingly.

Most of us don't normally bring these resources to the fore in our everyday lives, unless we expect some learning to take place. This state of mind alone is likely to make the most significant impact on your adaptation process.

Apply Three Ways to Gain Cultural Knowledge
There are three ways to gain knowledge of the culture around you: observation, communication, and study.

Observation
+ Allow yourself to be an observer for a while. At the beginning, you are likely to pick up and register in your mind the things that are done in similar ways in your homeland. Then you are likely to notice and even become very sensitive to the things that are different.
+ Observe and define the similarities and differences you find between the two cultures. Consciously making those comparisons in your mind will give you a better grasp of the features of the local culture.
+ Complete the Assessing Cultural Differences exercise on page 101 to help you identify the main cultural differences between the two cultures.
+ While you are observing the local culture, be aware that there are many minute details that you are not able to see. It takes time to see beyond the crude elements of an unfamiliar culture.
+ Remember that even similar behaviors to that of your homeland may carry different meanings for local people.
+ The media, national and public events, holiday celebrations, markets, fairs, rallies, concerts, sports, and games, are all great "live" learning experiences. They provide opportunities to observe some of the main values and norms of the host society as they come to life on these occasions. Take time to attend some events during your first year.

Communication

✦ Engage and communicate with local people. Be proactive: ask for the information you need instead of waiting for life to throw it at you.

✦ In most countries, local people will be more than happy to explain things such as holiday celebrations, the history of the country, or current affairs. However, they are not likely to be able to explain the inner workings of their own culture.

✦ The most effective cultural learning often occurs through other emigrants, or expatriates, who have been through the process of acculturation and are able to define the differences between the two cultures. Ask your countrymen to tell you about the local culture and to compare the two cultures.

✦ Anthropologists who study foreign cultures often work alongside a "cultural informant"—someone who is knowledgeable about the local culture and willing to share this knowledge. It is a useful way to learn about and connect with a new environment. Your mentor may be able to fulfill this role for you.

Study

✦ Study the culture. Many of the tourist attractions (museums, historical buildings and sites, and shows) are geared to help you do just that. This is a fun way to build your knowledge.

✦ Tourist and expatriate guidebooks, as well as children's books, can be very helpful in giving you an insight into the culture.

✦ Make it a priority to learn the local language. Language is the foundation of your cultural learning. See the recommendations in Chapter 7 regarding language training.

✦ When learning the language, be aware of the cultural context and the typical codes of behavior that accompany the communication.

Balance Exploration and Withdrawal

As we have seen, constantly being in an unfamiliar cultural environment and communicating in a foreign language requires mental effort and can be exhausting. It can also negatively affect your identity, your self-confidence, and your sense of belonging.

✦ To restore your morale and self-confidence, spend time on a regular basis with people you are comfortable with, who share your culture and language.

✦ Organize and structure your learning: focus on one topic at a time, and when you complete it, move to the next. It will also help you build your knowledge in a coherent way.

✦ Review what you have learned every day: share or verbalize your learning with other people, or write a relocation journal to document your learning.

Four Stages to Bridging the Cultural Divide

✦ Realize and accept that people in other places have developed different ways to deal with life events.

✦ Take time to study the local culture and the language.

✦ Compare the two cultures. This will better enable you to grasp and deal with the differences you observe.

✦ Learn to deal with people based on understanding their point of view, whether or not you agree with it.

ADAPT GRADUALLY

One of the main pains of cross-cultural adaptation is the apprehension that when we adapt to a new culture we change the essence of who we are. As we gain a deeper understanding of our host culture, we begin to adjust our actions and reactions. In this process we change aspects that are central to who we are: our behavior, manners, language, habits, values, way of thinking, networks, sense of belonging, and, indeed, our identity. The problem is that the new learning and the behavioral adaptation that follow are likely to make you feel inauthentic. This, in turn, generates self-resistance: your psyche tends to resist the changes. You may feel that when adjusting your behavior to the local style you betray parts of yourself.

✦ The best way to address this is to pace your adaptation to suit your comfort zone. Don't adopt behavior that makes you feel extremely uncomfortable, or causes you to lose your self-respect.

✦ Be aware that when you are learning a new way of doing something you do not discard the old way. You are simply adding to your repertoire.

✦ In time, you will learn to accommodate two cultures within you. As mentioned above, through the adaptation process we become bi-cultural. We learn to accommodate within us two cultures: two ways of thinking, two ways of making sense of the world, and two identities. The outcome of this process is cognitive and behavioral flexibility.

AN IMPORTANT TIP FOR SUCCESSFUL ADAPTATION
Do not become judgmental!
Cultures are not good or bad, inferior or superior.
They are just different.

RESPECT CULTURAL DIFFERENCES

✦ Don't assume that other people are "like us," and accept the differences between the cultures without judgment. Expect differences, and take time to learn and understand them.

✦ Remember that everyone has an ethnocentric tendency to think that his own culture is superior to all others. Yet, cultures are not better or worse than others; they are just different. The culture of your host country is simply a particular set of tools that has developed over centuries and helps these people to live their lives and solve their problems.

+ Once you understand that cultures have myriad ways to solve life issues, you are less likely to see only one way of doing things as "right."
+ See the funny side of cultural differences.
+ Cultivate a sense of humor and a capacity to laugh at yourself! You will need it from time to time.

How People Respond to Difference

+ **Ethnocentrism** is a view held by a person that the ways of life of his or her group or nation are superior to others, and all other cultures are judged as inferior.
+ **Naive-realism** is a person's belief that everyone else in the world sees life and interprets events as he or she does. For them there is only one reasonable explanation for everything—their explanation.
+ **Stereotyping** is extrapolating the cultural characteristics of only a few people to apply them to the whole of the group to which they belong. This is usually based on race, religion, ethnic origin, nationality, gender, socio-economic status, or other group affiliations.
+ **Ethno-relativism** is an approach that holds that cultures can be understood only relative to one another, and that a particular behavior can be understood only within its cultural context.

New Situations, or Situations That Don't Make Sense

These can be treated in three different ways:

+ **The colonialist way.** Colonialists do not react to the foreign culture. They ignore or eliminate these situations.
+ **The imperialist way.** Imperialists tend to force their own value system and way of thinking on to the new culture. They treat these situations as they would in their homeland, thereby taking the risk of drawing wrong conclusions.

✦ **The inter-culturalist way.** Inter-culturalists are fully aware of the complexity and ambiguity of exchanges in foreign cultures, and attempt to adapt by changing their thinking, and by trying to find a compromise between cultures. They are likely to admit that they cannot make sense of events and work to try to expand and modify their "typical" thinking.

Throughout the adaptation process it is important to guard against our natural tendency to be critical of cultural practices and attitudes that are different from our own. This tendency becomes even stronger when things are not going well.

While stereotyping may be temporarily satisfying to someone in the throes of culture shock, it is destructive and alienating in the long run.

CROSS-CULTURAL INCIDENTS

Cross-cultural incidents are clashes, misunderstandings, or conflicts that occur in cross-cultural situations. At the center of these incidents are cultural differences. When cross-cultural incidents occur, deeply held beliefs and expectations clash, and beliefs about what is "normal," "natural," "proper," "right," or "good" are challenged.

Such incidents frequently happen when rules of communication are broken, and when neither side recognizes that there is a misunderstanding or a misinterpretation that hampers the exchange.

When cross-cultural incidents occur, one party, and often both parties, may feel uncomfortable, offended, hurt, harassed, embarrassed, or threatened. Consequently, our attention is diverted from the interaction to how we feel, and this reduces our capacity to be attentive and focused. Therefore, the immediate outcome of cross-cultural incidents is that one or both parties may "shut down" and pull themselves out of interaction, with the common outcome that the newcomer isolates himself and turns against the local culture.

Realizing that cross-cultural conflicts are likely to occur and understanding what it is about cultures that causes such reactions go a long way to reduce conflict.

What Can Be Done?

✦ Don't assume that other people are "like us," and don't expect them to behave as you do. Expect them to be different, and take the time to understand these differences.

✦ Don't judge others according to your standards.

✦ Don't isolate yourself. Once you develop negative attitudes toward the local people you are likely to want to limit your contact with them, which slows down your adaptation process.

✦ If you interpret something negatively, seek clarification. Remember that your interpretation is colored by your cultural expectations, and may be wrong.

✦ If you think you have offended someone by miscommunicating your intentions, act with integrity and clear up the incident.

✦ You can choose to be hard on yourself when you get it wrong, or you can say, "All right, I got it wrong. That's OK. I am entitled to, I'm new here!"

Learning a second culture is not necessarily about becoming an expert in that specific culture. It is about your capacity to see the world through someone else's eyes, and to accept cultural differences.

As we have seen, the ability to function in another culture, and gain entrance into the cultural worlds of others, requires much more than knowledge of that culture. It requires the development of a cross-cultural outlook and behavioral flexibility. These skills are developed through experiential learning—ongoing engagement with the new culture, live experimentation, and reflective processes that enable you to gain the essential cultural knowledge and to apply it by adjusting your own behavior to your environment. It also necessitates an ability to regulate your own mental state, and tackle some of the trials of cultural adjustment, which we have reviewed here.

The cross-cultural adaptation process described here is a fascinating learning experience, and, as you will find, it is also an immensely enriching journey of self-discovery.

> Think of it this way:
> imagine we all have just one eye, and, suddenly,
> we are given a second eye. What will the
> second eye allow us to do?
> It will give us a perspective, and an ability
> to look more deeply, see more widely,
> experience things more vividly,
> and see things that we couldn't see before.
> This is exactly what the knowledge of
> another culture offers us.

Chapter 22

THE REWARDS OF SUCCESSFUL ADAPTATION

Cultural effectiveness comes at the cost of culture shock: heightened self-awareness, low morale, and continuous grind through the ups and downs of the adaptation process. It requires us to keep a close watch on our own mental state, resist our natural temptation to remain in your comfort zone, and avoid judging others before we have understood them.

There is no way around this: if you want to be truly successful in your overseas venture, then you have to become culturally effective. Yet, as we have seen, many people do not. They settle for being somewhat or occasionally effective, and lose out on the many rewards of successful adaptation.

Your task may seem daunting, but, as with any challenge that is worth taking up, the rewards are proportionate to the effort.

I believe that the rewards of cross-cultural journeys outweigh the costs, the risks, and the effort. Your appreciation of another culture, the new friendships you make, the life you witness, and your cross-cultural communication skills—these will remain with you for life. They may, however, permanently change the way you view the world.

The most obvious reward for being culturally effective is that it greatly increases your chances of accomplishing the goals you set when you decided to relocate. No one likes to fail, especially not in an undertaking of this magnitude, in which you invest months or even years of your life, and in which you incur significant losses on the way.

Another consequence of being culturally effective is the sense of security it allows you to feel. When you don't know which behavior of yours is appropriate and what is expected of you, you may err on the side of caution, constantly walking on eggshells. In this state of semi-paralysis, you cannot be very effective, simply because your attention and focus are not on the job, but on the details surrounding it. It is also exhausting.

Cultural ignorance is a breeding ground for fear and incompetence. Not knowing what the local people will do or how they will react produces constant tension and unease. You can never be altogether confident or comfortable, never free of the suspicion that what you do not know can hurt you.

The outcome of knowing the locals and their culture frees you to relax and be yourself again. When you understand the host culture and learn what is appropriate and what is not, you can stop monitoring yourself and can release your grip on your instincts. The relief that comes with authenticity is enormous.

An additional benefit of cross-cultural competence is that the better you understand the local culture, the harder it is for the locals to hide behind it. When you know the culture, you will be more able to distinguish between a situation that is caused by someone's personal sensitivity, and a cross-cultural incident that is caused by a cultural agenda.

Another great bonus of becoming culturally effective is the ability to see the world from a new perspective. You begin to take an interest in world affairs and develop a global perspective on the problems facing humanity. You develop the curiosity and passion for travel and discovery.

As you learn the details of another culture, you develop open-mindedness, tolerance, and the capacity to handle differences. You develop the ability to see the world from other people's point of view. This does not mean that you abandon your cultural perspective, but only that you are now able to see a situation, behavior, or attitude from more than one perspective. You understand that behavior that makes no sense to you may make perfect sense to others. As a result, you are not quick to judge others. You begin to tolerate opinions and actions that you may have dismissed before. You give others the benefit of the doubt, where previously you would not.

The ability to see situations, problems, practices—the way we do things—from multiple perspectives, or from the way other people see things, is a tremendous benefit to you and those around you. Whatever the circumstances, you can always see alternatives to the ordinary response. Isn't this what we mean by "thinking outside the box," "changing paradigms," and "reinventing yourself"? When you are overseas, this is what you do every day!

The realization that you are capable of such resilience, flexibility, and development is also an immense gift. People who know they can rise to the challenge—that they can adapt and endure the upheaval of culture shock—develop a can-do attitude that boosts and nurtures their lives.

Another benefit of learning about a new culture is that in the process we become aware of our own. At home, we are rarely prompted to reflect on our cultural selves—the parts of ourselves that have been shaped by the culture in which we grew up. But once we encounter a new frame of reference, we begin to see what we could not see beforehand. This inward journey is extremely important. It adds to who we are. Indeed, living abroad presents us with the opportunity for self-discovery and, thereby, self-improvement.

By far the greatest reward of becoming culturally effective is the doom it saves us from. The alternative is to live among people we don't understand and can't engage with, and therefore can never trust. It means living among people who repeatedly annoy and upset us, only to become critical and bitter. It means enclosing ourselves in the expatriate or emigrant community. It is a prescription for narrowing our world.

Tourists pay thousands of dollars for a brief glimpse of another culture, its history, traditions, and customs. Living abroad offers you a much richer, broader, and deeper experience, which is priceless.

As we have seen throughout this book, confronting a new culture and learning to live in a strange new environment is one of the most significant challenges you will ever face.

As you rise to the challenge, you will find yourself changing, adapting, and growing. And before you realize it, you become a seasoned traveler and an inter-culturalist: a citizen of the world.

TWO THINGS TO WALK AWAY WITH

There is Much to Learn
The relocation experience is, first and foremost, a learning experience. Much of this learning experience is about yourself. It is a fascinating journey of self-discovery.

The Gift of Curiosity
Keep your heart and mind open, and allow yourself to get excited! Develop an intense curiosity toward your new country, and toward your own journey of self-discovery.

Bon Voyage!

Appendix
Further Reading
Acknowledgments
Index

APPENDIX

THE RELOCATION JOURNEY AT A GLANCE

The following tables summarize the different phases of the relocation journey.

THE PRE-RELOCATION PHASES		
	THE DECISION PHASE	**PREPARATION AND PLANNING**
Timing	6-12 months prior to relocation	4-6 months prior to relocation
General attitude	Considering; Weighing up	Anticipation
Significant events	Collecting information; Inspection tour; Making the decision	Preparing; Planning
Emotional responses	Experiencing ups and downs: excitement and stress	High energy; Excitement; Fear of the unknown
Behavioral responses	Discussing and mulling over the topic	Planning and preparing to take action
Physical responses	Normal health; Possible insomnia	Normal health; Possible weariness or insomnia

THE PRE-RELOCATION PHASES (cont.)

	THE TRANSITION PERIOD	THE FAREWELL STAGE	THE RELOCATION DAY
Timing	6-8 weeks prior to relocation day	2-6 weeks before the relocation day	
General attitude	High gear; Energetic	Sadness	Mixed emotions
Significant events	Packing; Shipping; Selling; Moving	Informing others; Leaving work; Farewell party	Leaving home; Driving to the airport; Good-byes
Emotional responses	Sadness; Stress; Overwhelm; Anxiety	Concern and sadness about leaving family behind	Sorrow; Anxiety; Disbelief; Overwhelm
Behavioral responses	Withdrawal from current events; Distancing from others; Keeping busy	Gradual withdrawal from current activities and relations	Mixed emotions; Excitement; Tearing; Numbness; Irritability
Physical responses	Fatigue; Muscle ache; Insomnia	Normal health; Possible weariness and insomnia	Fatigue; Muscle ache; Insomnia

THE POST-RELOCATION PHASES

	THE HONEYMOON	CULTURE SHOCK
Timing	Starts upon arrival. Can last between a few days to several months.	Can occur immediately upon relocation or after the honeymoon phase. Can last between days to months.
General attitude	Excitement	Bewilderment; Impatience; Irritability; Moodiness
Significant events	Initial arrangements	Setting up new routines; Meeting new people; Everything is unfamiliar
Emotional responses	Exhilaration; Sense of adventure	Uncertainty; Doubt; Depression; Loss of confidence; Hypersensitivity
Behavioral responses	Curiosity; Exploring; Learning	Criticism; Hostility; Withdrawal into one's group
Physical responses	Unsettled health; Jet lag; Possible indigestion or insomnia	Unsettled health; Colds, headaches fatigue; Insomnia

THE POST-RELOCATION PHASES *(cont.)*

	RECOVERY	ADAPTATION AND GROWTH	INTEGRATION
Timing	Often begins during the first year. Can last for months.	Often begins during the second or third year. Can last for months or years.	Often begins during the third year. Can last for months or years.
General attitude	Acceptance	Energetic and positive; Open-mindedness	Belonging
Significant events	New friendships; Comfort zone	Normal performance restored; Adopting local customs	Adopting new identity
Emotional responses	Acceptance; Accommodation; Pride in oneself	Equilibrium; Adaptive energies	Calm; Confidence; Sense of place
Behavioral responses	Taking charge of life situations	Ready to learn and adapt	Constructive
Physical responses	Normal health	Normal health	Normal health

FURTHER READING

Bennet, M. *Basic Concepts of Intercultural Communication.* Boston: Intercultural Press, 1998.

Brayer Hess, M., and P. Linderman. *The Expert Expat, Revised Edition: Your Guide to Successful Relocation Abroad.* London: Intercultural Press 2002.

Byram, M., and A. Feng. *Living and Studying Abroad: Research and Practice.* Clevedon, UK: Multilingual Matters Ltd., 2006.

Byram, M., and A. Nichols. *Developing Intercultural Competence in Practice.* Clevedon, UK: Multilingual Matters Ltd., 2001.

The Culture Smart! series. London: Kuperard.

Fowler, S. *Intercultural Sourcebook: Cross-Cultural Training Methods.* Boston: Intercultural Press, 1999.

Geertz, C. *The Interpretation Of Cultures.* London: Basic Books, 1977

Hofstede, G. *Cultures and Organizations.* London: HarperCollins, 1994.

Hofstede, G. *Exploring Culture: Exercises, Stories and Synthetic Cultures.* Boston: Intercultural Press, 1994.

Kohls, R. and J. Knight. *Developing Intercultural Awareness: A Cross-Cultural Training Handbook.* London: Intercultural Press, 1994.

Landis, D., J. Bennett, and N. Bennett. *Handbook of Intercultural Training.* London: Sage, 2003.

Marx, E. *Breaking Through Culture Shock: What You Need to Succeed in International Business.* London: Nicholas Brealey Publishing, 2001.

Oberg, K. "Culture-shock: adjustment to new cultural environments," in *Practical Anthropology*, 7: 177-82, 1960.

Newcomer's Handbook Series. Portland, OR: First Books.

*Newcomer's Handbook Country Guide*s. Portland, OR: First Books.

Rogers, E. and T. Steinfatt. *Intercultural Communication.* Boston: Intercultural Press, 1998.

Thomas, D. and K. Inkson. *Cultural Intelligence: Living and Working Globally.* CA: Berrett Koehler Pub., 2009

Ward, C., C. Bochner, and F. Furnham. *The Psychology of Culture Shock.* Hove, UK: Routledge, 2001.

ACKNOWLEDGMENTS

The writing of this book has taken me many years of thought. It has involved conducting several studies on the relocation experience (including my Ph.D.), reading a mass of publications on the topic, developing materials for my own courses and workshops, training and counseling hundreds of clients and, finally, taking a break from everything to sit down and write it all.

First, I would like to thank my devoted husband Dan, and my fabulous children, Tal and Sharon, for their support and patience during the long hours I spent away from them to write this book.

Many other people have contributed to my thinking, and were invisible guides as the chapters of the book came together. Among them were my Ph.D. supervisor, Professor Stephen Ball, and my mentors and friends Professor Steve Gold, Professor Rina Shapira, and Professor Naama Sabar Ben-Yehushua, and my dearest friend, Dr. Flor Haymann.

I would also like to thank my close friends here in London, who have made a significant contribution to my thinking and writing since they have been through the relocation journey themselves; many of them have taken a key role in my own move, and have made a huge difference in my life. I thank them, and especially Miriam Chachamu, Haggit Inbar-Littas, and Miki Nathan for their ongoing support and encouragement.

I am immensely grateful to the friends and colleagues who were kind enough to review and comment on my book as it was coming together.

I would like to thank my course participants, trainees, clients, and research participants, who generously shared with me their relocation experiences and the lessons gained from them, and inspired me to write this book. Grateful acknowledgment is made for permission to use their narratives in the book. Pseudonyms have been used to protect their identities. Several stories have also been quoted from blogs and expatriate Web sites, and permission has been granted by the authors to include these in this book.

INDEX

FROM THE SAME PUBLISHER

CULTURE SMART!
The Essential Guides to Customs and Culture

Whether you are traveling for business or pleasure, the ability to understand other cultures is now accepted as essential. The *Culture Smart!* guides, published by Kuperard, reveal the human dimension of a country, providing visitors with a deeper understanding of the people they will meet. The series now covers more than eighty countries.

Written by authors who have gone through the process of cross-cultural adaptation themselves, these guides provide essential information on attitudes, beliefs, and behavior, ensuring that you arrive at your destination aware of basic manners, common courtesies, and sensitive issues. They cover the historical, political, and religious roots of local etiquette, and explain how your hosts may interpret the unprepared stranger in their midst.

The guides contain practical information on how to behave appropriately in various circumstances, and offer insights into the historical development of a country, its population, and local sensitivities. They cover areas such as: recognizing local religions, festivals, and holidays; native cuisine and dining etiquette; making friends; and social structures and family life. They encourage adapting to the local environment, understanding body language, and offer tips on forms of address and local manners. There is invaluable advice on how to stay safe, enjoy your experience, and not to offend your hosts.

·K·U·P·E·R·A·R·D·

In addition to the interested traveler, the *Culture Smart!* guides are particularly useful to government agencies and departments, language and training organizations, relocation agencies, travel and tourism companies, aid and relief organizations, students, and volunteer workers.

"The cultural guides offer glimpses into the psyche of a faraway world."
New York Times

"If you worry about being socially correct, you are likely to find Culture Smart! *a genuinely useful guide."*
Sunday Times Travel (London)

Countries in the series:

• Argentina	• Costa Rica	• Hungary	• Nepal	• Slovenia
• Armenia	• Croatia	• India	• Netherlands	• South Africa
• Australia	• Cuba	• Indonesia	• New	• Spain
• Austria	• Czech	• Iran	Zealand	• Sri Lanka
• Azerbaijan	Republic	• Ireland	• Nigeria	• Sweden
• Belarus	• Denmark	• Israel	• Norway	• Switzerland
• Belgium	• Dominican	• Italy	• Oman	• Syria
• Bolivia	Republic	• Jamaica	• Panama	• Tanzania
• Bosnia and	• Egypt	• Japan	• Peru	• Thailand
Herzegovina	• Estonia	• Kenya	• Philippines	• Trinidad and
• Botswana	• Ethiopia	• Korea	• Poland	Tobago
• Brazil	• Finland	• Libya	• Portugal	• Tunisia
• Britain	• France	• Lithuania	• Romania	• Turkey
• Cambodia	• Germany	• Malaysia	• Russia	• Ukraine
• Canada	• Ghana	• Mauritius	• Saudi Arabia	• UAE
• Chile	• Greece	• Mexico	• Scotland	• USA
• China	• Guatemala	• Morocco	• Singapore	• Vietnam
• Colombia	• Hong Kong	• Namibia	• Slovakia	

Each title is also available as an e-book.

For more information see
www.culturesmart.co.uk

FROM THE SAME PUBLISHER

DO I KNEEL OR DO I BOW?
**What You Need to Know When Attending
Religious Occasions**

Akasha Lonsdale

**Roman Catholic/ Protestant/ Orthodox Christian/
Jewish/ Muslim/ Hindu/ Sikh/ Buddhist**

ISBN: 978 1 85733 524 8

In today's multicultural society we are increasingly likely to form friendships and to work with people from a variety of religious backgrounds, and to find ourselves wondering about their beliefs and practices. How do they pray? What are their special days, feasts, or fasts, and how do they observe them? What foods do they eat, when, and why? We may even be invited to share their customs and celebrations.

To be invited into someone's personal religious world is a special honor, and one naturally wants to respond appropriately. Many questions arise. What should I wear, or not wear? Should I bring a gift? If so, what? What is happening in the service? Do I sit, stand, kneel, or bow? Should I hold back or join in? In short, how should a good guest behave?

This friendly, accessible guide provides an introduction to the major faiths—Western Christianity (Catholic and Protestant), Judaism, Islam, Hinduism, Sikhism, and Buddhism—and describes and explains the ceremonies in each that you may be invited to attend. It offers sensible advice on what to expect and how to behave on such